# Reading and Learning Difficulties

## Approaches to teaching and assessment

Peter Westwood

David Fulton Publishers

First published 2001 as
*Reading and Learning Difficulties*
by Australian Council for Educational Research Ltd
19 Prospect Hill Road, Camberwell, Victoria, 3124

Published in Great Britain (with amendments) in 2004 by
David Fulton Publishers, 414 Chiswick High Road, London W4 5TF

10  9  8  7  6  5  4  3  2  1

*British Library Cataloguing-in-Publication Data*
A catalogue record for this book is available from the British Library

ISBN 1 84312 196 4

Printed in Great Britain

# Contents

*To my very dear friend Mimi Lam Ching Yee*

# Preface

When, as a newly qualified teacher, I first began to take a professional interest in the teaching of reading in the late 1950s one could go to the relevant sections of a typical college or university library and find only a very modest collection of texts dealing with reading methodology and children's reading difficulties. Since that time, the literature published on children's reading development has grown exponentially, and any writer wishing to keep abreast of the field is faced with a daunting task. Hoffman, Baumann and Afflerbach (2000) quote the amazing statistic that since 1963 there have been over 25 000 research studies carried out and published in the field of reading. It is regrettable that only a few of these studies have had any real impact on teachers' beliefs and practices. Indeed, many teachers remain unaware of the important findings from reading research because it is not published in journals that are easily accessible to the profession.

In this small volume it is, of course, impossible to do justice to the wealth of knowledge (and *mis*information) available on the topic of teaching children to read, and on methods for assisting failing readers. I have chosen a path that represents best my own views and experiences, first as a mainstream teacher and then as special educator concerned for more than forty years with children who experience learning difficulties. I have made every effort to base my own teaching and writing firmly on research and classroom evidence of what produces the most effective outcomes for these children.

In writing this book I have tried to avoid entering into what has become known as the 'Reading Wars' (Stanovich 2000) – although I have not been entirely successful in this, as you will see. My own beliefs and experiences have led me towards a more balanced and structured approach to the teaching of reading than full acceptance of the whole language philosophy would ever allow. My interpretation of 'balance' is outlined in Chapter 4. I believe, for example, in the importance of explicitly teaching all children to use phonic knowledge and skills as an essential component of the reading programme. I do not believe that learning the alphabetic principle should be left to chance and given low priority in the classroom. Without mastery of phonic skills and an adequate sight vocabulary, children never reach the stage of automaticity in processing text that enables them to read confidently, fluently and critically. I also believe that most of the whole language principles provide an excellent framework and context in which to foster children's enjoyment of reading and writing. To me it makes sense to combine the best features of whole language approach with the necessary explicit teaching of component skills and strategies. That is the central theme of this book.

PETER WESTWOOD
HONG KONG, 2001

# Learning to read

Learning to read and write is arguably the most complex task humans face.
(Strickland 1999, p. xix)

It is clear that, for most children, the process of learning to read begins long before they enter school and receive instruction from teachers. Studies of preschool children indicate that if they live in a family environment where they observe adults or siblings using print materials and engaging in writing, they too will be motivated to engage in such activities. In literate home environments it is normal for stories to be read to children, and for them to be given books to own and explore. As a result, many quite young children begin to discover for themselves important concepts about reading and print (Adams 1990; Cunningham *et al.* 2000; Roberts 1999). Most young children will want to learn to read and write, and will soon begin to experiment with books and 'pretend' reading and writing. Their learning at this stage is mainly incidental, rather than the result of any formal or systematic teaching – although some wise parents intuitively engage their children in many types of informal teaching and learning interactions when reading and sharing books.

Researchers have referred to this early pre-reading stage as 'emergent literacy' (Burns, Griffin & Snow 1999; Foorman *et al.* 1997; Strickland 1990). Emergent literacy is defined by Sulzby (1991, p. 273) as, 'The reading and writing behaviours of young children that precede and develop into conventional literacy'.

## Emergent literacy

The period of emergent reading begins in the very early years of a child's life and extends into the first years of schooling. For some children with learning difficulties, or with developmental delay, the emergent reading stage may even extend into the middle primary years. Fields and Spangler (2000, p. 104) have remarked that, 'Schools would like it if all youngsters moved from emergent reading to independent reading during first grade, but it is totally unrealistic'.

The notion of emergent literacy, as a fairly natural developmental process, has largely replaced the earlier concept of 'reading readiness'. The old notion of reading readiness implied that children could not begin to learn to read until their latent perceptual and cognitive abilities were mature enough to enable them

My friend Kate has a dog called Spot. He is scared of thunder and litening, and when the whether is stormy he hides under Kates bed and no one can get him to come out

weather
wheather

to cope with the challenging task of reading (Cunningham *et al.* 2000). For many years the erroneous belief was held that a child must have a so-called 'mental age' of at least six years to be ready for reading. Such a belief has been discredited. The evidence is that many children learn to read in the preschool years (Adams, Treiman & Pressley 1998). A child's readiness to learn to read has much more to do with his or her prior learning experiences and opportunities than with physiological or neurological maturation.

As part of the emergent stage, even very young children begin to understand that books contain stories and pictures, and they show interest in looking at and handling books. They come to realise that print on the page conveys meaning to those who can 'read' and that 'readers' can convert this print into spoken language. They may develop an awareness that a story begins at the 'front' of the book and that the reader processes the print from left to right across and down the page while reading a story. Through fairly frequent exposure to books and stories (and perhaps as a result of watching children's educational television programs) some children begin to remember the shapes and names of letters of the alphabet, and may even begin to identify a few words. At the same time, they are learning to recognise commonly occurring signs, symbols and words encountered daily in their environment.

In terms of their auditory skills (*phonological skills*), many children are becoming aware that some spoken words rhyme and some words begin with the same sound. In their oral language they will often engage spontaneously in 'word play', creating rhymes or using alliteration. A few children will acquire a complete understanding that the words they say and hear can be 'stretched out' and said slowly so that each sound within the word can be heard (*phonemic awareness*). Many children, however, do not acquire phonemic awareness until specific teaching occurs when they enter kindergarten or school.

The pre-school children who are most advanced in their development, or who have had more direct guidance from someone as part of their exposure to books and print, begin to discover that there is a connection between the sounds in words and the symbols on the page of print (Barron 1994; Roberts 1999). In this respect, their early attempts to spell words as they pretend to write are extremely important. During the emergent spelling stage children attend more carefully to sounds within a word, and wonder how these sounds might be represented by letters.

Lyon (1998, p. 18) wrote:

> The evidence suggests strongly that educators can foster reading development
> by providing kindergarten children with instruction that develops print

concepts, familiarity with the purposes of reading and writing, age-appropriate vocabulary, language comprehension skills and familiarity with the language structure.

All this learning will, of course, be acquired more rapidly if an interested adult or sibling draws a child's attention to words, letters, sounds, rhymes, directionality of print and the format of a book when a story is being read or when he or she experiments with writing (Cunningham 2000; Schumm & Schumm 1999). The positive interaction between a competent reader and a beginner is a crucial factor in determining just how much young children learn during the emergent reading stage.

To summarise, the experiences young children encounter during the emergent reading stage should, according to Schumm and Schumm (1999), result in the following acquisitions:

- Story awareness – recognising that a story typically has a beginning, middle and end; usually has characters, and that the events in the story occur in times and places.

- Book awareness – recognising the basic parts of a book (cover, title, pages); knowing where a reader begins to read a story; understanding page turning; and so on.

- Print awareness – understanding the difference between letters and words; recognising where text begins on the page; knowing the direction a reader's eyes move when reading a line of print; gradually learning the names and common sounds (*phonemes*) associated with different letters.

- Phonological awareness – an understanding of words as separate units in speech (*word concept*); an ability to detect similarities and differences in speech sounds, and to detect alliteration and rhyme in speech; the ability to break spoken words down into separate sounds; the ability to blend sounds into words.

- Environmental print awareness – recognising signs, symbols and words that occur frequently in their environment (for example, street signs, product labels in stores or on television, name tags, logos).

## Moving beyond the emergent stage

Much more will be said about print awareness and phonological awareness later but at this point it is essential to dispel a possible misconception. It must not be assumed that because many pre-school children in supportive family environments learn so much about reading without any systematic teaching, they will also become proficient readers without direct instruction in school. Such a notion, according to Foorman *et al.* (1997 p. 246), is 'blatantly wrong'. While some children learn to read and write with remarkable ease even before commencing school, for the vast majority of children, proficient reading skills will not emerge naturally out of their oral and aural language experiences. In general, children do not learn to read by osmosis, they learn by being taught the necessary skills and strategies to identify words and make meaning from text (Adams, Treiman & Pressley 1998; Graves, Juel & Graves 1998; Lyon 1998; Turner 1995). They also require abundant opportunities to practise everything they learn.

Many children will not make a smooth transition from the emergent reading stage to independence in reading without a great deal of skilled teaching. This is particularly the case with children who come to school lacking awareness of stories, books, print and phonemes. Nicholson (1999) has summarised much of the research indicating that, if used alone, informal exposure to books and print will not ensure that all children acquire the knowledge and skills to become competent readers. Pre-school and early school exposure to books, and an opportunity to experiment with writing creates a very necessary, *but not sufficient*, condition to pave the way for independence in reading. High-quality instruction is also required.

## The importance of phonological awareness

Children's success in beginning reading is very highly correlated with their level of phonological awareness (Torgesen 2000; Tunmer & Chapman 1999). Phonological awareness is the general term used to describe an individual's understanding of the sound features of language. It includes an awareness that language utterances are made up of individual words, that words themselves are made up of one or more syllables, and that a syllable is made up of separate units of sound (phonemes). The language children hear everyday is perceived mainly as a continuous flow of speech, not as a sequence of word-units separated by breaks, as in printed language. Young children do not necessarily understand that 'words' exist as units in their own right (McGuinness 1998). Asking some children to 'look at the first word in the sentence' can be a totally meaningless instruction if word concept is not established. For this reason, one very important aspect of a young child's early development in phonological awareness is the acquisition of 'word concept' (Adams, Treiman & Pressley 1998). Until a child

appreciates that a word is a unit of speech there is little relevance in attempting to talk to the child about 'sounds within the word' or to attempt to teach any basic sound-to-letter correspondences. Children do not seem to benefit much from instruction in letter–sound correspondences until they possess an adequate level of phonological awareness (Castle 1999).

*Phonemic awareness* is the specific term referring to that aspect of phonological awareness involving the recognition that a spoken word is made up of a sequence of individual sounds. Phonemic awareness has nothing to do directly with print; it is the metalinguistic ability that enables an individual to identify sounds within words. Children need to be trained from the start to become aware of the individual phonemes in words because this understanding makes it very much easier for them to learn to read. Without phonemic awareness children will not be able to identify and discriminate among the various speech sounds – an essential first step in learning phonics (Rubin 2000). Snow, Burns and Griffin (1998, p. 52) describe the situation clearly:

> Because phonemes are the units of sound that are represented by the letters of the alphabet, an awareness of phonemes is the key to understanding the logic of the alphabetic principle and thus to the learnability of phonics and spelling.

Lack of phonemic awareness seems to be the start of a vicious cycle (Pressley 1998). Deficiencies in phonemic awareness undermine a child's ability to learn how to decode words. Poor decoding skill results in slow and frustrating encounters with print. This, in turn, undermines the successful reading and comprehending of a wide range of text. The result is children who do not enjoy reading, have little inclination to persevere and, when compared with their peers, engage in much less practice.

Phonological skills and practice in reading are considered to share a reciprocal relationship. Success in beginning to read appears to depend on having already acquired some degree of phonemic awareness; then, as a child reads more material and encounters many new words, so facility in decoding and phonemic awareness increases (Moustafa 2000; Perfetti *et al.* 1987). Children who read very little miss out on this opportunity to improve.

Phonemic awareness in young children has proved to be a more potent predictor of later reading success than measures of intelligence, vocabulary or listening comprehension (Castle 1999). Lack of phonemic awareness has also been identified as a probable causal factor in many cases of reading disability (Stanovich 2000; Torgesen 2000). This issue is discussed in more detail in Chapter 3.

Phonemic awareness develops most naturally from the many and varied oral and aural language interactions that occur in the family and in the preschool or early school environment. In particular, children may well have acquired phonemic awareness without specific instruction if they have had many stories read to them, have listened to and recited rhymes, played games such as 'I spy' and attempted to spell words while pretending to write. Other children may have been less fortunate and will require direct teaching in order to establish this core concept (Nicholson 1999; Pressley 1998). Children from restricted language backgrounds are most at risk of failing to discover the phonological characteristics of their language.

## Examples of phonemic skill

The various aspects of phonemic awareness usually thought by researchers and educators to be important for reading development are:

- recognising rhyme (bat, fat, sat, hat, mice, dice, rice, price);
- identifying the initial sound in a word (house = /h/; tree = /tr/);
- being aware of alliteration (greedy green gremlins);
- being able to count or clap syllables in a word (/Mon/ - /day/);
- blending a sequence of phonemes to make a word (/pr/- /o/ - /d/ = prod);
- being able to break single syllables into onset and rime units (truck: /tr/ = onset, /uck/ = rime);
- breaking words down into a sequence of phonemes (pram = /p/- /r/- /a/ -/m/);
- manipulating sounds to form different words (rake can become bake; mat can become map; set can become sit).

Some researchers have identified more phonemic skills than those listed above. There is also some debate concerning the sequence in which the various phonemic skills are acquired. Differences in prior language experience may result in differences in the order in which children acquire the various skills.

Of the phonological skills listed above, breaking a word down into its separate phonemes (segmenting) and combining phonemes to pronounce words (blending) appear to be the best predictors of reading progress. They are also the most closely related to the process of decoding words in print (McGuinness 1998).

The concept of rhyming appears to be important for linking sound patterns to the letter patterns (phonograms) that occur within similar words (*cake, make, flake, shake*). Awareness of these common letter patterns is extremely important for both word identification and spelling purposes (Dombey 1999). This is discussed in more detail in Chapter 6.

Many well-controlled studies of the effects of training children in phonemic awareness show conclusively that for optimum impact on reading skills, phonemic training needs to be accompanied by explicit instruction in the relationships between phonemes and the letters used to represent them in print (phonics). McGuinness (1998) and Gunning (2001) mount a convincing case for beginning phonics teaching with the sounds and mapping from speech sounds to letters, rather than the reverse process, as is often the case in letter–sound instruction. Moving from words to sounds, and then from sounds to letters, allows the teacher to begin with meaningful material rather than abstract symbols. For example, the teacher might say, 'What sound do we hear at the beginning of the word *monkey*? *Mmmm*onkey. Yes, it's the /m/ sound. This is how we write 'm'. Let's think of some other words beginning with the /m/ sound. Can you find two more things beginning with /m/ in this picture? You write the letter 'm' on each one.'

Phonemic awareness and basic phonic skills should never be taught in totally decontextualised ways. While the relationships between phonemes and letters are being acquired, children need to apply this knowledge to word identification when reading meaningful connected text (for example, Bus & van Ijzendoorn 1999; Foorman *et al.* 1998; Lovett *et al.* 2000; Teale & Yokota 2000).

## Learning the alphabetic code

Entry into print depends on understanding how the writing system works and then learning to use it efficiently. The writing system works on the alphabetic principle; namely, that spoken words can be reduced into component sounds and that these sounds are represented in print and writing by certain letters or groups of letters. Discovering, or being taught, the alphabetic principle is the key to successfully learning to read and to spell (Byrne 1998; Ehri 1998; McGuinness 1998).

For a complete understanding of how an alphabetic writing system works children must have a thorough grasp of the following:

- the ability to analyse words into phonemes;
- an understanding that phonemes occur in all words;
- knowledge of which letter symbols represent which phoneme;
- awareness that there is a fairly consistent (but far from perfect) relationship between each phoneme and letter across all positions in a word.

In order to become skilled readers, children must learn correspondences between letters or letter groups and phonemes and must apply this knowledge to identify words. In other words, phonic *knowledge* must be converted to phonic *skill*. There are some children with learning difficulties who appear to know basic letter-to-sound correspondences but they do not use this knowledge in any systematic way to decode unfamiliar words.

### Phonic skills

'Phonic skill' refers to an individual's ability to apply knowledge of letter–sound relationships to reading and spelling words. Phonic skill represents the most powerful tool to help children become independent readers (Rubin 2000; Strickland 1998). Acquisition of phonic skill is particularly important in the beginning stages of learning to read and write. Phonic decoding strategies are also utilised by mature readers and writers when they encounter difficult or unfamiliar words.

Many teachers seem to equate phonic knowledge and skills simply with knowing the common sound units associated with the single letters of the alphabet. Phonic knowledge certainly includes this very basic level but it extends beyond this to include an understanding that some sound units in speech need to be represented by a group of letters (for example, bl, ch, tr, str, squ, tion, and so on.), and also that the same sound unit may be represented by more than one letter group (for example, ite and ight). When this principle is understood by a reader, a much higher proportion of English words become decodable (Dombey 1999).

Some reading methodology experts are now recommending that children be taught almost from the beginning how to recognise letter groups, rather than spending too long practising decoding from individual letters (for example, Cunningham 2000; Gaskins 1998; Graves, Juel & Graves 1998; Gunning 2000; Gunning 2001). In particular, teaching rimes (phonograms), prefixes and suffixes can be helpful. Gunning (2001) states that teaching letter groups as pronounceable word-parts is very effective because that is the way that children naturally try to decode words (for example, from onsets and rimes). It is also argued that this recognition of letter groups facilitates a child's future ability to make analogies between familiar and unfamiliar words (Moustafa 2000).

Most of the harsh criticisms of phonics teaching in the past stemmed from the fact that it was often done in a decontextualised manner, frequently through the medium of rather boring workbooks and routine exercises. Current practice is to teach phonics and word study from the vocabulary encountered in meaningful reading and writing activities. There is unanimous agreement among all advocates for the teaching of phonic skills that as far as possible such teaching must be an integrated part of a meaningful literacy programme, not something done in isolation (Bear *et al.* 2000; Cunningham 2000; Ehri 1997; Gunning 2001; Harrison 1996). This principle does not *totally* preclude the teaching of word-attack skills and spelling through the use of word families and vocabulary lists, but all such learning needs to be applied immediately to authentic reading and writing activities. Some teachers devote time to intensive word study and phonics through the use of 'mini lessons' within the main language and literacy programme.

Approaches to the teaching of phonic skills are discussed in Chapters 4, 5 and 6.

## Sight vocabulary

One essential component of speed and automaticity in reading is an extensive vocabulary of words recognised instantly by sight. These words are often referred to as 'sight words' or 'sight vocabulary'. Being able to read many words automatically by sight contributes massively to fluent reading and is the most efficient way to unlock the meaning of any text (Ehri 1997). Reading a word by sight, however, does not mean necessarily that the whole word is stored as a complete image, merely that important clusters of letters characteristic of that word are stored and can lead to its instant recognition (for example, vocabu ...).

The term 'basic sight vocabulary' is often used, and refers to a child's knowledge of the one hundred or so most commonly occurring (high-frequency) words. Many of these very common words are not 'regular' in their sound-to-letter translations so must be acquired by a visual memory approach (Dombey 1999). Many exposures to high-frequency words result in children storing in long-term memory the key components of each word's orthographic pattern. When the words are encountered again in connected text they are instantly identified from a perception of significant sequences of letters within the word.

Children who possess phonic knowledge appear to learn sight words much more easily than children who use only a 'look-and-say' strategy (Cunningham 2000). Letter knowledge clearly aids storage of orthographic patterns. On this matter Gunning (2001, p. xii) observed:

> I noticed that the time-honoured practice of having students memorize a store of high-frequency words wasn't working. Without any systematic way to attach sounds to letters, the students quickly forgot the words they memorized. Once they were taught phonics to help them remember the words their performance improved significantly.

When discussing children with limited sight vocabulary, Nicholson (1998, p. 188) wrote:

> If these children were able to read quickly and accurately then the extra mental energy saved by not having to struggle with each word could be applied to comprehending what they read, which is what reading is all about.

For this reason, helping children with reading difficulties build their sight vocabulary needs to be given high priority. Increasing children's reservoir of sight words aids the development of overall automaticity in processing print (Thompson 1999).

Sight vocabulary grows with increasing reading experience. As children encounter and decode more and more new words over a long period of time, these words also become part of sight vocabulary. This fact provides yet more validation for the vital role played by regular, sustained reading practice.

## Comprehension

It is generally agreed by educators that, even in the earliest stages, comprehension must be the central focus of teaching children to read and not something to be emphasised only after children have learned how to decode and identify words (Teale & Yokota 2000). Even in the beginning stages of reading acquisition, children should discuss, reflect upon, ask and answer questions about what they have read or what has been read to them. It is never too early to develop critical readers.

Most definitions of reading stress that it is a process of getting meaning from print. Understanding information in the text is, of course, the whole purpose of reading. A cognitive-constructivist view of reading emphasises that it is a process in which readers actively search for and make meaning for themselves in what they read (Gambrell & Dromsky 2000). The message in any text cannot be absorbed passively by a reader. It requires sustained cognitive effort on the reader's part.

Reading comprehension has been described as 'a complex intellectual process involving a number of abilities' (Rubin 2000, p. 171). Readers must use information already acquired to filter, interpret, organise, reflect upon and establish relationships with the new incoming information on the page. In order to understand text, a reader must be able to identify words rapidly, know the meaning of almost all of the words and be able to combine units of meaning into a coherent message. Understanding of text results from an interaction between word identification, prior knowledge and the effective use of cognitive strategies (Lyon 1998; Scarborough 1998).

Children who are good comprehenders use a variety of cognitive processes as they read. They may:

- pose mental questions to themselves and seek answers in the text;
- generate visual images when reading certain types of material, particularly narratives;
- mentally summarise the main points in a key paragraph;
- reflect upon and consider the importance or relevance of what they have read.

Readers who understand what they are reading can more easily go beyond the given information on the page in order to predict, infer and make connections.

Good readers almost always have some personal feelings or reactions to what they are reading. They are 'active' readers in the sense of becoming involved cognitively and emotionally in what they read (Cunningham *et al.* 2000). They are keen and interested in using text as a way of obtaining information, learning new ideas, solving problems and as a source of enjoyment. Children who don't understand much of what they read are likely to turn away from reading as it provides no satisfaction. According to Torgesen (2000), reading comprehension is thus a cognitive, motivational and affective activity.

## Comprehension strategies

Pressley (1999) says that good comprehenders are effective users of comprehension strategies when they work with text. A strategy can be defined as a mental plan of action designed to achieve a specific purpose. One of the priorities in any reading program is to teach children, particularly those with reading difficulties, a range of strategies to use to extract meaning and evaluate information from texts. There is also an obvious need to provide abundant opportunities for these strategies to be practised, using a broad range of texts.

Effective comprehension requires that the reader maintain the meaning throughout the reading of the text. If meaning is lost, the reader should be aware of this fact immediately and take necessary compensatory action. Strategic readers use metacognition to monitor their own level of understanding as they read. Often they will modify their approach to the text in the light of their own self-monitoring (Hoffman & McCarthey 2000). They may, for example, pause to go back and read again a particular sentence or paragraph or they may check the meaning of a word in the glossary.

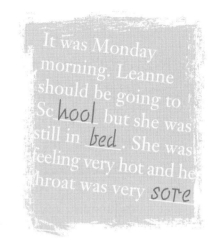

Pressley (1999) argues that the goal of teaching should be to develop fully self-regulated readers who are skilled and strategic. He challenges the opinion, held by many teachers, that children will improve in comprehension ability if they simply do massive amounts of reading practice. Pressley suggests that *strategy training* should be an essential part of any balanced approach to literacy teaching. Magliano, Trabasso and Graesser (1999) cite numerous research studies indicating that comprehension can be improved by strategy training. Examples of comprehension strategies and how they may be taught are presented in Chapters 2 and 5.

# 2 The reading process

> Skilled reading is a highly complex capability involving many component processes and extensive knowledge. (Gagne, Yekovich & Yekovich 1993, p. 269)

In order to determine the type of instruction children need, it is important first to consider what is actually involved in the process of reading and comprehending text. Such basic information provides clear pointers to what children need to be taught. An understanding of what is involved in reading also helps to identify possible causes for a child's reading difficulties (see Chapter 3).

## What does skilled reading involve?

Having reviewed the extensive research literature on reading and reading difficulties, Burns, Griffin and Snow (1999, p. 88) reached the conclusion that:

> For a child to read fluently, he or she must recognize words at a glance, and use the conventions of letter–sound correspondences automatically. Without these word recognition skills, children will never be able to read or understand text comfortably and competently.

Pressley (1998) agrees, and suggests that to become competent readers children need to learn two things: word identification strategies and comprehension strategies. These two sets of strategies are very closely interrelated, with comprehension being heavily dependent upon a reader's swift and efficient identification of the words on the page. To some extent, word identification and comprehension share a reciprocal relationship. Rapid word identification obviously facilitates and supports understanding, and reading with understanding promotes speed and fluency in processing print (Rayner, Rayner & Pollatsek 1995). Effective literacy instruction must include a planned programme for the explicit teaching of both word identification skills and comprehension strategies to enable children to read fluently, with enjoyment and understanding (Strickland 1998; Torgesen 2000).

Word identification is the most obvious area of difficulty exhibited by children with reading problems (Lyon 1998; Nicholson 1998).

## Accurate word identification

It may seem self-evident that reading involves the fast and efficient recognition of words, but in the past there has been heated debate on this particular issue. The debate concerns the extent to which skilled readers actually do (or do not) attend to the details of words and letters. On the one hand, research studies have yielded incontrovertible data over the years to show that reading, at all age levels, does require the reader to process the print very carefully (for example, Adams 1990; Adams, Treiman & Pressley 1998; Ehri 1997; Just & Carpenter 1987; Stuart *et al.* 1999; Rayner & Pollatsek 1989; Thompson 1999; Torgesen 2000). On the other hand, advocates of the meaning–emphasis or 'whole language' approach to reading acquisition argue that skilled reading is mainly a 'psycholinguistic

guessing game' in which the reader merely skims the text for important clues that convey the general meaning of the paragraph and support the reader's predictions (Goodman 1996). They believe it is the search for 'meaning' that drives the process of reading, rather than any careful visual perception of letters and words. Advocates for the meaning–emphasis approach (for example, Cambourne 1988; Goodman 1986; Smith 1979; Weaver 1994) suggest that learning to read is more about becoming skilled in predicting the words on the page than becoming skilled in attending closely to the letters and engaging in any form of decoding. They place maximum faith in a reader's ability to use prior knowledge of the subject matter, together with an awareness of language structure, to derive the essential meaning of a text without needing to look closely at every word. Indeed, Goodman (1997, p. 4) insists:

> Readers sample selectively from the print using their knowledge of the writing system. They do not process each feature of each letter of each word. Rather they use their experience to select the most useful information and infer the rest.

'Whole language' principles and practices are discussed in detail in Chapter 4.

The issue of whether or not skilled readers process text at the level of letters and words, or whether they operate in a rather different way to make meaning, is fundamental to an understanding of the reading process and the way reading skills should be taught from the beginning. If readers need to become highly skilled and efficient in word and letter recognition, then teaching the appropriate knowledge and strategies for decoding and word identification should be given high priority. If the meaning–emphasis theory is correct and they do not really need to devote their attention to accurate word recognition and decoding, then perhaps teachers should be encouraging beginning readers to attend mainly to contextual cues.

# Eye movements and reading

It is pertinent to refer briefly to research that has examined the eye movements of readers while they reading. It is obvious that if the whole language advocates are correct, then a reader's eyes will merely skim the text and occasionally come to rest on important contextual cues. These eye movements will be very different from those of a reader who carefully and systematically processes the words and sentences line by line in order to derive the meaning.

The studies of eye movements have proved conclusively that even skilled and mature readers do attend to almost every word in every line in the text (Balota & Rayner 1991; Dunn-Rankin 1985; Fisher & Shebilske 1985; Liubinas 2000; Rayner, Rayner & Pollatsek 1995). Only very short functional words such as conjunctions, articles and prepositions are sometimes ignored or partially ignored. The eye-movement research confirms that a good reader engages in very careful and systematic visual processing of print. The reader's eyes do not skip around the page to sample for meaning and look for contextual cues, as the whole language exponents suggest. The studies do not support the theory that we read mainly by guessing, but rather that we read by carefully identifying the words on the page (Dymock & Nicholson 1999; Harrison 1996; Rayner 1997).

It is true that as we read our eyes do not move steadily and smoothly along the line of print from left to right, but move along the line in a series of rapid jumps (saccades) and pauses (fixations). We do not register any useful information during the saccade, but we take in important visual information during the fixation (Rayner 1997). The letters at the focal point of the fixation (in the 'foveal region') are perceived most clearly and they usually convey the information that leads to immediate word recognition. Although we fixate on most words in the line, we do not need to fixate on each and every word. The perceptual span within a normal fixation allows us to perceive clearly up to approximately eight letters to the right of the fixation, within what is called the 'parafoveal region', as well as up to four letters to the left (Balota & Rayner 1991; Pavlidis 1981; Rayner, Rayner & Pollatsek 1995; Ryan 1999; Underwood & Batt 1996). Perceiving some of the letters in the next word may assist with prediction of that word without the need to fixate on it. There are also occasional 'regressive movements' of the eyes back again to an early word to check or confirm. With all readers, skilled and novice, these regressive sweeps are more frequent when the text is difficult. Very frequent regressive eye movements and much longer times spent on each fixation are common in beginning readers and in children with reading difficulties, even when they are reading quite simple text.

Skilled readers carry out this visual processing with amazing speed and efficiency. Beginning readers and those with learning difficulties do so much more slowly and by expending much more mental effort. The challenge for teachers is therefore to help all children become more rapid and automatic in word identification since this skill is the prerequisite for effective comprehension (Harrison 1996). For effective reading, readers need to recognise words and assign meanings swiftly and automatically (Graves, Juel & Graves 1998).

## How words are recognised

A word can be identified by:

- retrieving it from memory (sight words and sight vocabulary);
- sounding out the letters and then blending the phonemes to produce the word (that is decoding followed by encoding – alphabetic principle and phonic skills);
- recognising and pronouncing a group of letters representing a known 'spelling pattern' or pronounceable unit within a word (that is a more advanced form of decoding – orthographic stage);
- comparing the word, or parts of the word, with a known word (reading by analogy);
- using context to predict the word (syntactic and semantic cues).

As readers gain experience, they become capable of reading words in all five ways listed above thus developing speed, fluency and confidence. Proficient readers tend to use multiple sources of information simultaneously, some related to meaning and context, some to prior knowledge and experience, others to letter–sound connections (Church, Fessler & Bender 1998).

The recognition of a word involves both visual–perceptual and cognitive processes. According to Cunningham *et al.* (2000), skilled readers perceive almost all the letters or letter-groups in a word during a visual fixation. Becoming fluent and swift at word identification mainly involves making relevant connections between the letter strings within words and the sound units they represent. What the brain does is recognise instantly any familiar groups or patterns of letters. As a result of previous reading experience, these letter patterns have become associated with pronounceable parts of known words and the images are stored in long-term memory. Using information provided by the letter patterns, most printed words can be identified very swiftly by the skilled reader, usually within 300 milliseconds (Pavlidis 1981; Rayner, Rayner & Pollatsek 1995). In the case of all familiar words, recognition and meaning are registered simultaneously. Any words not read before will take slightly longer to decipher but are usually identified from their pronounceable spelling patterns or by decoding them letter by letter (Adams 1990). All words that are encountered frequently enough become stored in memory as 'sight words' and no longer need to be decoded.

The capacity to store these important images without conscious effort is referred to as 'orthographic memorisation' (Thompson 1999). The letter patterns stored as images are termed 'functional graphemic units' (for example, -ious, -oot, br-, -tt, tre-, stri-) (Ehri 1997). In the case of small, high-frequency words (for example, she, it, the, in) the whole word may be stored as an image. Readers with a good store of orthographic images can use this information to identify new words (Rumsey & Eden 1998).

The evidence seems to be that children making normal progress in learning to read begin quite quickly to store letter patterns that will help them to work out other words. Children with learning difficulties have much greater problems storing and retrieving these important units of information.

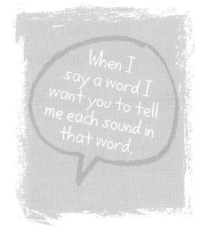

In the case of very young children, and older children with reading difficulties, the processes described above are rather different. The fact that they have not yet established a useful store of visual images of familiar words and commonly occurring letter patterns makes it necessary for them to spend much more of their time trying to identify each new word from its separate letters.

## Reading difficulties and vision

It is not uncommon to find that a teacher believes a child's reading difficulty is due to problems with eyesight but the vast majority of reading difficulties are not caused by vision impairment or by visual perceptual anomalies (McGuinness 1998). This is not to say that in individual cases of learning failure vision may not be implicated in some way.

Ryan (1999), for example, discusses possible subtle dysfunctions in visual perception that might cause difficulties in rapid processing of sequentially arranged stimuli, such as letters in a word, but this is not suggested as a frequent or common cause of reading failure. Some studies have reported abnormal eye movements in individuals with reading difficulties. The general consensus is, however, that rather than being a cause of reading difficulty, unusual eye movements may be the result of a poor reader's limited ability in word recognition and the way he or she is trying to compensate (Critchley 1981; Howell & Peachey 1990). As stated above, poor readers make many more regressive eye movements than do good readers, and they are likely to spend longer in each fixation while they process a word. For most children, these aspects of performance improve as they engage in more reading and writing activities.

It is also worth noting that some vision experts have suggested that any teaching methods requiring a very young child to learn words by sight (the so-called 'look and say' approach) should not be used. It is said that many young children starting school do not have the perceptual attention span needed to capture sufficient information for a sight-reading approach (Liubinas 2000). Harrison, Zollner and Magill (1996), for example, report that a significant number of young children (possibly one child in three) may have a very restricted visual attention span, making it impossible for them to perceive and learn words as wholes.

Learning to decode using letters and small letter groups obviously suits this characteristic of children's visual-processing ability at that age.

## In-text supports for word identification

In addition to the letter patterns of the words themselves, there are other sources of information within the text that help a reader to identify words with speed and accuracy. For many years reading experts (for example, Adams 1998; Fox 2000; Goodman 1967; Kemp 1987; Stanovich 1980) have suggested that three main cueing systems are used interactively in the identification of words. The three systems involve support from meaning (semantic cues), grammar and language patterns (syntactic cues), and letter–sound correspondences (grapho-phonic cues).

### Semantic cues

These cues come from the meaning of what we are reading and help us to identify and confirm words. When we are understanding most of what we are reading, our knowledge of the subject matter is likely to guide our expectations for the words appearing on the page. This type of cueing is often referred to as 'contextual support'. When used along with information from the initial letter or letters within the word, context does assist with word identification (Thompson 1999).

### Syntactic cues

These cues enable us to draw upon our experience of language. We use what we know about normal sentence structure and grammar to help us recognise or predict a word. For example, 'The tiny mouse *dragged* the cheese back to her hole'. The word underlined must be a verb. Is it took, dragged, carried, moved, pulled, pushed? We are helped to make an instant decision by additional cues from the letters. As the eyes focus on the word 'mouse' most of the letters in the next word to the right are also perceived within the same fixation. We are aware that the up-coming word begins with 'dr' and that it contains two 'gg's, so we are likely to settle on 'dragged'.

### Grapho-phonic (or alphabetic) cues

Information about sound-to-letter relationships enables us to decode an unfamiliar word and deduce its possible pronunciation. This is the only strategy that can help us if the word is not supported by context or by the sentence structure. As Dombey (1999, p. 53) observes, 'Without a sound working knowledge of grapho-phonics, readers have no efficient way of identifying new words or storing their existing word knowledge.' To make use of grapho-phonic cues the reader needs to have developed phonic decoding skills (see below).

Advocates for the whole language approach to reading place maximum importance on the semantic and syntactic cues because they are directly related to understanding what is being read, and to familiarity with natural language patterns (Marzano & Paynter 1994). It can be seen in the explanations above, however, that a knowledge of letters and letter–sound relationships significantly enhances both the syntactic and semantic sources of information. It is this knowledge, not context, that provides the *main* driving force behind accurate reading (Adams 1998). Fox (2000, p. 11) comments, 'Though the syntactic and semantic cues are rich, if you want to be absolutely certain about the word, you will turn your attention to cues that are a combination of how words look and sound.' Similarly, Thompson (1997) comments that, when attempting unfamiliar words, context may provide some useful information but only in combination with the reader's use of information from letter–sound correspondences. Rather than being typical of skilled and fluent readers, it tends to be beginning readers and others lacking adequate word identification skills who have to resort to guessing from context clues (Lyon 1998; Nicholson 1991). Teaching children to attend mainly to meaning cues, and to guess rather than process the letters in the word, is teaching them an immature strategy most closely associated with inefficient reading (Carver 2000; Pressley, 1998). Overall, the conclusion is that the efficacy of contextual guessing as a principal strategy for reading has been greatly overestimated and misinterpreted (Share & Stanovich 1995).

Prior (1996) indicates that all children need to become fully proficient in decoding words from phonic information provided by letter symbols. She says that once a child can do this he or she has a means of working out the pronunciation of all English words. Fluent readers use the code automatically so that the reading process is smooth and relatively effortless. They also build up a repertoire of words they can recognise instantly by sight.

## Word identification: stages in development

Other complementary views of the word identification process have attempted to identify separate stages of development in the reader. For example, Frith (1985) suggested that an individual's word recognition capability seems to progress gradually from a holistic approach in the beginning stage to an increasingly analytical strategy. Frith uses the terms logographic, alphabetic and orthographic to classify three main stages.

### Logographic stage

Words are recognised from their general appearance. They are remembered as a pattern of letters and sometimes from *idiosyncratic* visual features such as word length or size and style of print. Children may acquire a large sight vocabulary during this visual logographic stage but they have not realised that the letters in a word are in any way an aid to its pronunciation. Dombey (1999) indicates that children who have difficulty with the alphabetic code will continue to treat the writing system as if each word were a separate logogram (an idiosyncratic assembly of letters to be memorised as a whole) rather than as a code that can be converted to sounds.

### Alphabetic stage

The decoding of a word takes place using a knowledge of letter-to-sound correspondences. As already noted, this stage depends on children first having a good understanding that spoken words can be broken into smaller units of sound (phonemic awareness) and that these sounds are represented by the letters.

### Orthographic stage

Words are identified by attending to larger clusters of letters. Letter strings that frequently occur are recognised in different words; features such as prefixes, suffixes and roots that signal meaningful (morphemic) units are recognised. As described earlier, swift, efficient reading is accomplished by the ability to process words from immediate recognition of relevant parts of their overall spelling pattern. It is at this stage that a reader becomes able to read unfamiliar words, or parts of words, by analogy with other known words.

Ehri (1997) identifies very similar stages in the development of word recognition but subdivides the alphabetic stage into *partial alphabetic*, in which the reader is just beginning to link sounds to certain letters (for example, initial letter; final letter) and *full alphabetic*, in which a working knowledge of all single letters, digraphs and blends is used to decode unfamiliar words. Ehri (1997) refers to the final orthographic stage as *consolidated alphabetic*. At this stage the reader is able to recognise multi-letter units that represent syllables, morphemes or pronounceable parts of words. This latter stage is achieved only after abundant practice with and exposure to text and involves making relevant connections between letter groups and speech units (Ehri 1998).

Recognising words swiftly and efficiently is only a means to achieve the main purpose of reading for meaning. Effective reading comprehension strategies and the factors influencing ease or difficulty with which a reader obtains meaning from text will now be considered in detail.

## Comprehending text

It is essential that reading comprehension be seen as something that begins as early as the beginning of reading and not something that children move on to after they have learned to decode print. Even before children can read, the adult usually asks children questions about stories that they have just had read to them. 'What was the giant's name?', 'What might the little girl do next?', 'Which part of the story did you like best?', 'Did you feel sorry for the old lady?' When children get older and more advanced in their reading, discussion of the text and questioning are still essential ways of developing comprehension and study skills (see Chapter 5).

Browne (1998) reminds teachers that children's previous experiences as speakers and listeners and as participants in story readings lead them to expect that the information in books will make sense. Skilled readers use their knowledge and experience of the world, language, books and subject matter, in conjunction with the words on the page, to make meaning when they are reading.

## Levels of comprehension

Reading comprehension is considered to occur at four levels of complexity. These levels are often referred to as literal level, inferential level, critical level and creative level (Smith 1969). Consider the following brief passage:

> For the seventh time that week Miss Chow took the lift down to the ground floor where the landlord had his office. She was glad that she did not have to walk down the stairs as her flat was on the 10th floor. She knocked on the office door and went in. The landlord did not look pleased to see her.
>
> 'They are playing their music at full blast *again*,' she complained. 'Those people in 10B. What are you going to do about it?'
>
> The landlord sighed and rubbed his eyes. 'Look, Miss Chow. I will do what I can. This seems to go on all the time. I can understand how you feel, but they take no notice of me and there is nothing in their lease to say they can't play music. If all else fails, you could move up to the flat on the 18th floor. That will be vacant after next week. It has the best views of the harbour and it's the best flat we have. How about that?'

### Literal level

At the literal level the basic facts are understood. For example, knowing that the lady's name is Miss Chow; she lives in a flat on the 10th floor; her neighbours are noisy; she has complained to the landlord before. This information is contained explicitly within the text.

### Inferential level

At the inferential level the reader is able to go beyond what is written on the page and add meaning or draw conclusions. For example, Miss Chow believes that her landlord will tell the neighbours to be less noisy, that he will sort the matter out for her. It can also be inferred that things may not improve even if the landlord does complain. The reader also gathers that the landlord is becoming a little frustrated or irritated by Miss Chow's complaints.

### Critical level

At the critical level the reader assesses the good sense of what he or she is reading, its clarity, accuracy and any apparent exaggeration or bias. For example,

when Miss Chow's landlord offers her a different flat on the 18th floor and says it is the best flat, with the best view of the harbour, the reader knows he could be exaggerating. Critical and inferential reading together probably make the reader feel that moving up to the 18th floor may not suit Miss Chow and it is not a good solution.

**Creative level**

At the creative level the reader can take information or ideas from what has been read and develop new ideas from them. The creative level stimulates the reader to new and original thinking. For example, the reader comes to understand that landlords should write a clause in their leasing agreement to say that if the tenant makes noise and the landlord receives complaints, the tenant will be asked to leave within one week. The reader might also be able to suggest other ways of dealing with Miss Chow's problem; or might write a short story indicating what happens next time Miss Chow is disturbed by her neighbours.

## A strategic approach to comprehension

Children who are effective comprehenders usually consciously or unconsciously apply a system for extracting meaning from text and evaluating critically what they read (Pressley 1999). They have a mental plan of action designed to achieve a specific purpose. For example, the basic strategies readers might use to assist with the processing and understanding of text include:

- carefully previewing and overviewing what is to be read;
- self-questioning (What do I know already about this? Do I agree with this point?);
- selectively reading some sections of text deeply and skimming other sections;
- identifying the main ideas;
- ignoring redundant information;
- rehearsing information they may want to recall later;
- re-reading difficult or important sections;
- reflecting and thinking critically about the information;
- summarising the main points and relevant detail.

The specific cognitive strategies listed above are those usually taught to children within a strategy-training programme. The positive benefits of comprehension strategy training are well supported by most research studies (Kavale & Forness 2000; Swanson 1999). Some examples of specific strategy-training approaches are presented in Chapter 5.

Some children with poor comprehension may be quite adequate in word identification but lacking any systematic way of processing the information on the page. These children seem often to have no effective text-processing strategies that they can use consistently and appropriately. Such children are suitable candidates for intensive strategy training.

## Factors influencing reading comprehension

A reader's understanding of text is influenced by a broad range of factors, including his or her motivation, interest, vocabulary, general knowledge, knowledge of the particular subject, word identification skills, reasoning ability, use of effective strategies to identify main ideas and supporting detail, and an appreciation of text structure (Torgesen 2000). Reading with understanding involves the smooth co-ordination of higher order cognitive processes (thinking, reasoning, analysing, connecting, reflecting) and lower order processes (word recognition, decoding) (Pressley 1998).

Some children are poor comprehenders because they lack fluency in lower order reading processes. For example, slow reading caused by inefficient decoding very seriously impairs the understanding of text (Carver 2000), while fluent reading normally enhances it (Teale & Yokota 2000). In the case of good readers, automaticity in word recognition allows short-term cognitive capacity (working memory) to be devoted almost entirely to comprehension. Conversely, a lack of automaticity in word recognition or decoding causes short-term cognitive capacity to be overloaded or used inefficiently as the reader searches for contextual or other clues to help identify the words.

Children with limited vocabulary have comprehension difficulties for obvious reasons; they do not know the meanings of many words on the page, unless the text is very simple. Birsh (1999) indicates that reading comprehension is closely related to a child's oral language comprehension and vocabulary.

# 3 Learning difficulties

Most children who rely on schooling to learn to read and who receive good reading instruction do, in fact, become successful, lifelong readers. However, there are some children for whom good instruction is necessary – but not enough. (Burns, Griffin & Snow 1999, p. 127)

Reading is a very complex skill and for this reason it is not surprising to find that some children encounter difficulties in learning to read. The number of children failing to reach a satisfactory standard of literacy has been a matter of some concern in the United States, Britain, New Zealand and Australia. Efforts to improve literacy skills in some countries have resulted in national initiatives such as specific policies and government directives on literacy teaching, regular monitoring of literacy standards, 'whole school approaches' to support children with literacy problems, the introduction of a daily 'literacy hour' in schools and increased attention given to early identification and intervention for children at risk of failure.

## Children with literacy problems

The exact prevalence rate of children with significant learning difficulties in literacy is open to debate. In Australia it is estimated that at least 16 per cent of the school population shows such problems (Prior 1996). Using a broader category, 'children with learning difficulties' as a criterion for identification, most estimates tend to range from a low of 10 per cent to a high of 20 per cent (Rivalland & House 2000), with some sources putting the figure even higher at 25 per cent to 30 per cent (House of Representatives Standing Committee 1993; Nicholson 1994; Rivalland 2000; Westwood & Graham 2000).

The actual number of children with reading problems differs quite significantly from school to school, with some schools identifying very few such children, others reporting many. Literacy standards seem to be most problematic in schools serving lower socio-economic neighbourhoods (Snow, Burns & Griffin 1998). Birsh (1999) indicates that within the population of poor readers there is a disproportion of children from low-income and minority groups and from groups where English is the second language.

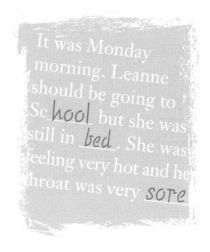

## Possible causes of reading difficulty

What causes some children to experience difficulty in learning to read? The simple answer to this question is that many different factors contribute to a learning problem. Some factors are located within the learner or the learner's background, some within the teaching approach, some within the learning environment, and some are possibly related to the working relationship between teacher and student. It is very rare indeed to find one specific reason to explain why a child fails to learn to read, even after extensive diagnostic and psycho-educational assessment.

### Teachers' perceptions

Teachers themselves are not particularly skilled in recognising the cause of a child's learning difficulty. They may know a child is having problems but they are unable to find out why. Teachers often assume that the cause of any learning difficulty lies within the child or his or her family background (Cheng 1998; Westwood 1995). Many teachers believe that reading problems are caused by genetic factors, physiological or neurological 'deficits', maturational delay, minor sensory handicaps or impairments in psychological processes such as memory and perception or a 'learning disability'. Some teachers believe that the problem is due to a child's poor attitude and motivation, linking this sometimes with lack of educational support from the home. In almost all cases they tend to 'blame the victim' rather than question the quality and quantity of the teaching the child receives in school (Allington 1998). The problem with subscribing to this 'deficit model' of reading difficulty is that it lowers a teacher's expectations of the progress a student might make if given extra assistance. The 'blame the victim' approach can prove to be a self-fulfilling prophecy.

It is important for teachers to understand that most reading problems are not necessarily due to any so-called 'deficits' within a child. This erroneous impression may have been created, perhaps, by the very heavy focus given to neurological, perceptual and cognitive factors in the literature on learning disabilities. While these within-the-learner factors do contribute to the learning problems of *some* children, they are not the primary cause of most cases of reading difficulty. McGuinness (1998, p. 220) states categorically that, 'Children fail to learn to read in school because they aren't being taught correctly.' Similarly, Cunningham *et al.* (2000, p. 299) suggest that many more children are 'instructionally disabled' than are 'learning disabled' – a view they support with classroom evidence.

The suggestion that poor teaching may be the sole cause of a learning difficulty may be a slight over-statement; but at least it compels us to consider factors over which we have more control (for example, curriculum, teaching methods and time allocated to learning).

## Teaching methods, curricula and learning difficulties

It is now believed that some children experience learning problems in literacy because they are not given sufficient explicit teaching of the essential knowledge and skills necessary to decode print (Harris & Graham 1996; Kameenui & Simmons 1999). Contemporary 'constructivist approaches', for example, place the onus on children to acquire knowledge and skills, largely through their own efforts, rather than being instructed directly and systematically by the teacher. In the domain of reading, constructivist approaches are based on the premise that children will learn sight vocabulary, phonic principles, decoding skills, spelling and comprehension strategies indirectly, through engaging daily in meaningful projects requiring the application of reading and writing skills. The role of the teacher in this context becomes that of a facilitator and supporter of children's efforts, rather than an instructor clearly imparting essential information. Constructivists tend to frown upon direct teaching, considering such 'transmission' methods to be 'old-fashioned'.

Unfortunately not all children can cope successfully with teaching methods that require them to learn without much teacher direction (Graham & Harris 1994; Mastropieri, Scruggs & Butcher 1997; Pressley & McCormick 1995). Some children appear to make better gains in literacy learning when teaching is direct and explicit. Research has strongly supported the view that direct teaching is a highly effective approach, particularly for teaching basic academic skills such as reading to children with learning difficulties (Birsh 1999; Kavale & Forness 2000; Swanson 1999).

## The importance of a successful start

The teaching approach used in the beginning stage of reading instruction is of paramount importance. A child needs to get off to a good start because success tends to build on success. A successful entry into the world of reading makes a child feel confident and intrinsically motivated. Failure quickly causes frustration, loss of confidence and avoidance.

Unfortunately, the evidence shows quite clearly that for some children a cycle of reading failure begins very early in their school careers. They do not get off to a smooth start and they typically fall behind more and more each year as their problems become compounded (Strickland 2000).

## The impact of early failure: affective factors

It is probable that no child ever approached the beginning stage of reading with a negative attitude. All young children want to be able to read. Negative attitudes only begin to develop when the child fails and becomes confused. Children who repeatedly fail may begin to believe they are incapable of success so they lose confidence and motivation (Rasinski & Padak 2000). They rapidly assume that reading is much too difficult for them and they believe they will never manage to do it, no matter how much extra help they are given. They often become passive and dependent learners, unwilling to take a risk and needing to be told what to do at every step (Graves, Juel & Graves 1998).

As Prior (1996) indicates, feelings of defeat are likely to cause such children to give up trying and develop a picture of themselves as 'failures'. It is possible that many children labelled as 'learning disabled' are actually displaying a type of learned helplessness in the face of a task that they don't fully understand (Hallahan & Kauffman 2000). They may have no perceptual or cognitive problems – they simply have not grasped how spoken language relates to the written code of letters and words on the page. They have had their confidence, self-esteem and eagerness to learn undermined by early failure. As a result, they have become resistant to assistance and developed effective avoidance strategies. If asked, they are likely to say that they hate reading because, for them, it entails such a great mental effort and gives so little satisfaction in return (Critchley 1981; Høien & Lundberg 2000). In general, they will try to engage as little as possible in reading and in doing so they negate the potential benefits of sustained practice. This situation is very difficult to rectify.

Given these very important affective influences on learning to read, the primary aim for the teaching of any child with a learning difficulty is to help that child become a more confident, effective and self-regulated learner. Assisting children with learning difficulties requires more than simply 'skills' training. Rasinski and Padak (2000) recognise this problem and advise that instructional planning for children with reading difficulties must give high priority to restoring confidence and maintaining positive attitudes towards reading.

Other educators (for example, Johnson 1998) draw attention to the importance of assessing children's motivation to learn and their reaction to persistent failure. Johnson suggests that teachers need also to be sensitive to children's emotional response to any extra help they may be given. For example, some children may strongly dislike coming out of the classroom to attend special reading lessons because it draws public attention to their difficulties. Some may not like working at that particular time of day (for example, after-school-hours tutoring). Others may find the additional burden of extra tuition too much to manage on top of their general school workload. These negative feelings will need to be addressed as they can present significant obstacles to a child's willing participation in tutorial sessions. Children's beliefs about their own capacity to improve their reading skills are also extremely influential in determining their attitude towards to extra tuition.

## Specific areas of difficulty

The most obvious problem that all children with reading difficulties exhibit is a serious deficiency in swift and accurate word identification (Burns, Griffin & Snow 1999; Manis, Custodio & Szeszulski 1993; Pressley 1998; Torgesen 2000).

This problem is due to several contributory factors including poor phonic skills, a limited sight vocabulary and inefficient use of context to support word recognition. Slow and inaccurate word identification leads directly to the second most obvious weakness, poor comprehension.

In order to examine these difficulties in more detail it is relevant to consider some of the underlying areas of knowledge and skill that are necessary to support word identification and the understanding of text. The general problem areas having impact on these aspects of reading can be summarised as follows (Chan & Dally 2000):

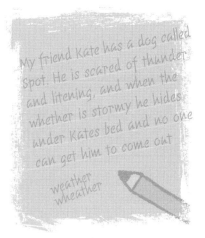

- language and metalinguistic problems;

- phonological processing problems;

- word recognition problems;

- text-processing problems.

These four areas are not mutually exclusive. Difficulties in one area frequently spill over into one or more of the other areas. For example, weaknesses in aural–oral language tend also to delay acquisition of phonemic awareness and limit vocabulary development. This, in turn, makes phonic decoding and word identification difficult to achieve. Poor word identification then impairs the reader's ability to understand what is being read.

## Language and metalinguistic problems

The broad category of language and metalinguistic problems includes learner characteristics such as:

- restricted vocabulary;

- poor syntactical awareness;

- limited memory span for verbal material;

- difficulty in rapid naming (or mental 'word-finding');

- weak listening comprehension.

All these factors have a negative impact on the fluency of reading and the understanding of what is read (Torgesen 2000). In particular, weaknesses in syntactical awareness, vocabulary and verbal memory reduce the opportunity for children to make effective use of semantic and syntactical cues when reading – although guessing from context is the strategy they are most likely to try to use if their phonic skills are weak. General language delay almost always retards the acquisition of important metalinguistic skills such as 'word concept' and the ability to segment words into component sounds. It should be noted, however, that poor phonemic awareness is not always attributable to poor oral language development. Phonological problems can be found in some individuals who have perfectly normal oral language development (Høien & Lundberg 2000).

The importance of oral language for early reading development is widely recognised. Children with any form of language delay are at risk of experiencing learning difficulties in reading. Screening tests for oral language have long been regarded as very useful in identifying such children (Flynn & Rahbar 1998; John 1998; Scarborough 1998) and most early intervention programs for literacy include a significant emphasis on listening and speaking activities.

In many cases, deficiencies in vocabulary, language awareness and aural comprehension may simply reflect a child's inadequate preschool language experience. In such cases, essential features of any literacy intervention program will be active stimulation of language development through oral work, discussion, listening to stories and asking and answering questions. Listening, talking, reading and writing will need to be given equal emphasis.

One rare type of severe reading disability (a sub-type of dyslexia) is considered to be a manifestation of an innate 'language disability' (Høien & Lundberg 2000). In these cases, difficulty in acquiring normal language proficiency may be constitutional. The children involved are often identified from a history of very late or abnormal speech development in the preschool years and from continuing immaturities in their structure and functional use of language (Prior 1996; Scarborough 1998). Any intervention program designed to help a child in this situation with his or her reading and spelling in school will benefit greatly from input and advice from a speech and language pathologist.

In all cases where language difficulties are believed to underpin a reading problem, the implication is clearly that language enrichment must be included as a top priority within the remedial reading and writing programme (Vaughn, Bos & Schumm 1997). In some cases this will be done to overcome a possible specific language disability but for the majority of children with literacy problems it will be to compensate for inadequate prior learning.

## Phonological processing problems

In Chapter 1 attention was drawn to the importance of well-developed phonemic awareness as a basis for children's understanding of the alphabetic code and learning phonic skills. Many studies have confirmed that children with literacy learning problems very frequently exhibit poorly developed phonological skills (Adams *et al.* 1998; Castle 1999; Tunmer & Chapman 1999; Wolf *et al.* 1994). Children with these phonological problems experience great difficulty in acquiring and applying sound–symbol information to help them identify words. This problem, in turn, causes difficulty in building a functional sight vocabulary (Gunning 2001). The most severe forms of reading disability (dyslexia) are often considered to be due almost entirely to a serious weakness in phonological processing (Siegel 1998; Torgesen, Wagner & Rashotte 1997).

It was also explained in Chapter 1 that phonemic awareness and reading skills share a reciprocal relationship. As a child successfully learns to read, he or she will also be gaining a great deal of additional insight into the phonemic structure of words. Children who are very poor readers, and read very little, do not have this same opportunity to gain additional phonemic knowledge from extensive reading experience. Chan and Dally (2000, p. 164) reach the conclusion that, 'deficits in phonological awareness can be both a cause and a consequence of reading difficulties'.

It can be appreciated that the inclusion of phonemic awareness training is usually essential in any early literacy intervention programme. Such training may also be needed within a remedial approach used with older readers if assessment has shown significant weaknesses in this area. Tests and procedures exist to enable teachers to determine any student's current phonological skills (see Chapter 7). Assessment helps in the planning of appropriate activities directed towards any areas of weakness (for example, blending, segmenting).

Early intervention involving the teaching of phonemic awareness, blending, and alphabetic knowledge has proved to be very effective in reducing the number of children who experience difficulty in the first two years of school, with more than 50 per cent of such children managing to return to a normal rate of learning (Torgesen 2000). However, there appears still to be a hardcore of some 2–4 per cent of problem readers who continue to have difficulty, even after intensive intervention. Their problems may stem from additional weaknesses described under the subheading 'dyslexia' (see p. 33). Clay (1997), while supporting fully the value of phoneme awareness training, suggests that it is not the only important component in remedial reading programs, and used alone it may not meet the needs of some problem readers.

## Weak phonic skills

In addition to weak phonological awareness – and often as a direct result of such weakness – many children with reading difficulties also display very poor phonic decoding skills. This deficiency prevents them from swift and confident identification of words. Tunmer and Chapman (1999) have cited research showing that failing readers with poor phonemic awareness are much less likely to discover letter–sound relationships for themselves simply from exposure to books. For these children, direct teaching of phonic knowledge and follow-up practice are required.

As stated in Chapter 1, some children with reading difficulties may know the common letter–sound correspondences from previous teaching, but they do not seem to use this knowledge in any systematic way when faced with an unfamiliar word. They may not have had sufficient successful experience in using the decoding strategy to have confidence in its value. The teaching of phonic decoding skills must therefore extend well beyond instruction in basic letter-to-sound correspondences. It must provide abundant opportunity for a child to apply phonic knowledge successfully to the decoding of many different words in order to build confidence in the decoding strategy. At the beginning stage, when a child needs to acquire the decoding skill, some experts recommend the use of reading material specifically designed to contain a high proportion of decodable words (for example, Kameenui & Simmons 1999).

## Word recognition problems

It has been stated already that one of the main characteristics of efficient reading is swift and accurate recognition of the words during each visual fixation. This speed and efficiency arises from two sources of information – an extensive sight vocabulary and an ability, during each fixation, to perceive letter sequences as familiar orthographic patterns. Poor readers do not possess an extensive basic sight vocabulary (Nicholson 1998). This is due in part to lack of reading experience and in part to lack of phonic knowledge (Gunning 2001). One obvious goal for intervention is to increase, by any means possible, a poor reader's sight vocabulary. The student needs to know a core list of the most commonly occurring words and should be able to read these words in context and out of context with a high degree of automaticity.

When I say a word I want you to tell me each sound in that word.

Children with weak phonological skills and limited phonic knowledge have great difficulty in reaching the level of word recognition that Frith (1985) called the 'orthographic stage' and Ehri (1997) describes as the 'consolidated alphabetic stage' (see Chapter 2). They exhibit a serious limitation in the number and range of words they can recognise as orthographic units (Manis, Custodio & Szeszulski 1993; Torgesen 2000). This deficiency causes them to continue to process print slowly and laboriously letter by letter, and they take many more repetitions than normal readers to begin to recognise words. Ehri's (1997; 1998) research confirms that children with a reading disability seem unable to memorise the important spelling patterns. Instead, they are cued mainly by the initial and final boundary letters – an inaccurate approach to word recognition, more typical of the earlier partial alphabetic stage.

## Text-processing problems

Poor readers often have difficulty in fully comprehending the text they are reading. Too much of their mental effort is drained by the lower-order processing of print or by inaccurate contextual guessing. They seem unable to orchestrate the various strategies required for identifying words and extracting meaning. Chan and Dally (2000, p. 165) clearly describe the basic problems:

> Whereas good readers become fast and accurate at recognizing words without context and within context, poor readers often remain dependent on context. The use of context to identify unfamiliar words and the labour-intensive efforts of poor readers to decode words, due to deficits in either

phonological or orthographic processing, tax the limited resources of working memory. When the lower level skills of word recognition are not automatic less attention is available for comprehending the meaning of text. The problems of lack of reading fluency (demands on working memory to hold words of a sentence long enough to derive its meaning) and effortful recognition of unfamiliar words compromise higher order processes such as comprehension and learning from texts.

In addition to the problems described above, poor readers tend not to self-monitor for understanding. Walker (2000) even suggests that some problem readers seem to lose sight of the fact that what they are reading is supposed to make sense; so when it doesn't make sense they make no attempt to self-correct. Many poor readers do not progress easily above the literal level of comprehension and encounter extreme difficulty in operating at the level of inferring, predicting, questioning, reflecting and criticising. To operate at these levels requires that lower order processes such as word identification are occurring automatically, thus releasing cognitive capacity for the higher order demands of comprehending the text.

The difficulties for most poor readers are compounded by the fact that they do not possess, and are not aware of, effective strategies to help them extract meaning. They do not have any mental plan of action to help them find main points, important details and key concepts or to form conclusions. They just tackle the print head-on. They do not think deeply about what they are reading and do not interact cognitively with the information. This makes any progression above the literal level of understanding difficult to achieve. Research suggests, however, that children can be taught effective comprehension strategies (see Chapter 5) and can become more confident in their own ability to tackle text successfully (Kavale & Forness 2000; Pressley 1991; Swanson 1999).

## Dyslexia

The word 'dyslexia' actually translates as 'difficulty with words'. More than a century ago, a school medical officer in England, W.P. Morgan, first described what he called a case of 'word-blindness' (cited in Doris 1998, p. 4). The case related to a 14-year-old boy, considered intelligent by his teacher, very competent in most school subjects, but who appeared to be almost totally incapable of learning to read, despite good teaching. To this day, that simple description fairly accurately covers the children now classified as 'dyslexic'. Over the years other terms have been used – specific reading disability, specific reading retardation, reading disorder, developmental dyslexia – to identify a sub-group of problem readers who are qualitatively different from other children who experience difficulties in becoming literate. In the words of Shapiro (1998, p. 22):

> One of the fundamental precepts of dyslexia is that affected children learn differently from children whose reading difficulty derives from low intellect. This latter group of children has been referred to as 'garden variety' poor readers.

The term dyslexia is currently applied to a severe and chronic form of reading difficulty found in children of normal intelligence (and sometimes of high intelligence). These children encounter major difficulty in learning to read, write and spell, even when exposed to efficient teaching and a supportive home background. They have no overt sensory or intellectual impairment and there is no obvious reason for their difficulties. Hallahan and Kauffman (2000) refer to them as an enigma. There is every reason, based on the children's apparent potential ability, to anticipate that they will learn to read easily – but they do not.

Identifying the cause or causes of dyslexia has been an important focus for research in the field of learning disabilities for many years. It has attracted the interest of neurologists, ophthalmologists, medical practitioners, speech pathologists, psychologists and, of course, teachers. Some studies over the years have implicated genetic factors (for example, Smith *et al.* 1998), central nervous system dysfunction, including abnormal processing within the cortex (Kaufmann 1996; Rumsey & Eden 1998), slow neurological maturation (Critchley 1981), visual perception difficulties (Ryan 1999), phonological deficits (Torgesen, Wagner & Rashotte 1997), and a 'dual deficit' comprising poor phonological skills together with slow retrieval of information from verbal memory (Wolf & Bowers 1999). Despite the vast amount of research data, it has been stated that, 'the cause of dyslexia is unknown; however, it is believed to be a combination of physiological, neurological and genetic factors' (Connel 1999, p. 10). In most individual cases of dyslexia the cause of a particular child's learning problem often remains a mystery (Hallahan & Kauffman 2000).

For many years, particularly since the 1960s when Kirk (1962) first coined the term 'learning disability', there have been major problems in reaching consensus over a precise definition of a learning disability or of dyslexia. Due to these problems with definition, exact prevalence figures for dyslexia are impossible to confirm. The prevalence rate appears to be within the range 1–10 per cent of the school population, with a figure of 4 per cent appearing most frequently in the official literature (for example, American Psychiatric Association 1994; AREA 2000; National Health and Medical Research Council 1990). If the strict criterion of 'at least average intelligence' (IQ 90 or above) is applied in the identification of dyslexic children, a lower figure of between 1–3 per cent is probably a more accurate estimation (McCoy 1995). Relative to other forms of reading difficulty, dyslexia is a fairly low-incidence disability and the term 'dyslexic' should not be applied to the majority of failing readers.

It is usually reported that many more boys than girls are dyslexic but some evidence suggests that the number of girls and boys with reading problems may be almost equal (Birsh 1999; Pressley & McCormick 1995). Girls tend not to draw attention to their learning problems in school and are not so easily identified by their teachers. Boys tend to develop overt and negative behaviours if they are experiencing difficulties and are more likely to draw attention to themselves.

## Definitions of dyslexia

Many definitions of dyslexia have been proposed over the years. One of these definitions was formulated in 1994 by the Orton Dyslexia Society Research Committee in the United States (cited in Johnson 1998, p. 138):

> Dyslexia is one of several distinct learning disabilities. It is a specific language-based disorder of constitutional origin characterized by difficulties in single word decoding, usually reflecting insufficient phonological processing. These difficulties in single word decoding are often unexpected in relation to age and other cognitive and academic abilities; they are not the result of generalized developmental disability or sensory impairment. Dyslexia is manifest by variable difficulty with different forms of language, often including, in addition to problems with reading, a conspicuous problem with acquiring proficiency in writing and spelling.

Earlier definitions tended to identify dyslexia as a distinct disability simply by excluding possible factors that might cause a reading problem. For example, in the 1960s the Research Group on Developmental Dyslexia of the World Federation of Neurology (cited in Ott 1997, p. 3) defined 'specific developmental dyslexia' as:

> a disorder manifest by difficulty in learning to read despite conventional instruction, adequate intelligence and socio-cultural opportunity. It depends on fundamental cognitive disabilities, which are frequently constitutional in origin.

This definition was widely accepted for many years within most of the disciplines dealing with learning disability (neurology, psychology, pedagogy). These earlier definitions tended not to describe the precise nature of a child's problem beyond the obvious difficulty in learning to read. The focus in the new definition has changed to include a more precise statement indicating exactly what it is the dyslexic student cannot do efficiently, namely decode words due to problems in phonological processing. Along the same lines, Høien and Lundberg (2000, p. 9) proposed a more concise and precise definition, suggesting  that dyslexia is 'a persisting disturbance in the coding of written language, which has as its cause a deficit in the phonological system'. These writers state that the dyslexic student is unable to develop the reliable, automatic decoding and encoding ability that is the chief characteristic of good readers.

Interestingly, Høien and Lundberg consider that a child of any intellectual level can be dyslexic. This perspective is different from the traditional criterion of 'at least average intelligence' that has formed an essential part of most earlier definitions and has usually been applied in selecting children for research purposes. The suggestion does accord, however, with the earlier views of

Pavlidis (1981) who argued that since dyslexia is caused by constitutional factors it should be encountered at all levels of intelligence.

## Possible sub-types of dyslexia

Dyslexic children do not form a homogeneous group (Castles & Coltheart 1993). About the only thing they share in common is the difficulty in achieving  reading and writing skills commensurate with their age and ability level and a weakness in phonic skills. The heterogeneity within the dyslexic population has created great interest among researchers and educators alike and has led to a search for distinct sub-types of dyslexia. It is believed that if sub-types and their unique learning characteristics can be identified, then teaching methods and materials can be tailored to suit a child's learning needs (Feagans & McKinney 1991). Much of this early work on sub-typing was carried out in the 1970s (for example, Bannatyne 1971; Boder 1970; Denckla 1972), but interest in this area continues.

Many studies have attempted to identify sub-types based on particular profiles of strength and weakness obtained when a child is given a comprehensive battery of perceptual, motor and cognitive tests (Doris 1998; Shapiro 1998). Others have looked for characteristic profiles on an individual intelligence test, such as the WISC–III. In the past, the results from these studies have sometimes led to tentative conclusions that the learning problems of dyslexic children are due either to weaknesses in auditory processing (phonological or auditive sub-type) or to poor visual perception (visual or dyseidetic sub-type). In some cases, children appear to have combined deficits in both phonological and visual processing and might form a 'mixed' sub-type.

Unfortunately, although a huge amount of effort has gone into the search for reliable sub-types, most of the research has produced conflicting and confusing results, yielding very little of practical value for improving early identification or for tailoring teaching intervention (Høien & Lundberg 2000; Stanovich *et al.* 1997). As Ott (1997) points out, dyslexic children do not fall neatly into a small number of different sub-types, and inconsistency is the main feature of their difficulties.

## Significant research findings

Other types of research in the field of learning disability have produced less conflicting results. In some cases of dyslexia, the child's literacy problem seems to be part of a more general 'language disability', with symptoms including late speech development, continuing problems in receptive and expressive communication and poor phonological skills (Høien & Lundberg 2000; Vellutino 1977). It is important, however, to stress that language-based difficulties simply cannot explain *all* cases of dyslexia. A significant number of intelligent dyslexic children are first identified by their teachers and parents simply because their oral verbal skills are *remarkably good* (Ott 1997).

Weaknesses in phonological processing, particularly phonemic awareness, are found in the vast majority of dyslexic children (Siegel 1998; Torgesen, Wagner & Rashotte 1997). However, phonological difficulties may not be the sole contributing cause in some cases of reading disability (Clay 1997).

Dyslexic children (and others with reading problems) have a major difficulty in attaining the 'orthographic' (awareness of common letter strings) level of word recognition (Torgesen 1999). This may be due to the fact that they have come to rely too much on guessing words from contextual cues, rather than attending closely to the words themselves. Or it may be a reflection of their weak phonic skills forcing them to decode words slowly letter by letter, rather than attending to more significant letter groups. Failure to attain the orthographic level of word recognition can also be the product of limited reading practice. The outcomes are a very slow and frustrating rate of reading and failure to build sight vocabulary.

Naming-speed problems appear to be a deficit in dyslexic children. Many of these children exhibit great difficulty in immediate retrieval of spoken vocabulary from long-term memory (Fletcher *et al.* 1997; Wolf 1997). For example, when dyslexic children are shown familiar visual stimuli (for example, common objects, colours, digits, letters) they are slower than other children to name the stimuli. This rapid-naming deficiency (sometimes termed 'dysnomia') impacts upon reading skill because it impairs the acquisition of fluency and automaticity. Wolf *et al.* (1994, p. 143) observe:

> An extensive body of cross-sectional and longitudinal evidence on English-speaking children indicates that the single most noted characteristic of poor readers outside their reading impairment is naming-speed problems: that is, deficiencies or disruptions in the processes underlying the precise, rapid access and retrieval of visually presented linguistic information.

Wolf and Bowers (1999) hypothesise that children with a naming-speed deficiency (possibly due to some minor but significant neurological inefficiency) may take longer to discriminate letters and words and to identify their sounds or meanings. This results in frustratingly slow reading speed and a significant difficulty in ever reaching the stage of using orthographic patterns for swift and easy word recognition. Lack of fluency also disrupts comprehension and makes reading a less-than-enjoyable activity.

In the most severe cases of dyslexia there may be a 'double deficit' operating – slow naming speed, together with major phonological difficulties (Berninger 1995; Wolf 1997; Wolf & Bowers 1999).

## Is the concept of 'dyslexia' useful?

Having described some of the current perspectives on dyslexia, it is necessary to point out that not all educators agree that this form of learning disability or syndrome exists separate from the general problems experienced by children in learning to read, write and spell (for example, Franklyn 1987; Education Department of Western Australia 1984; Prior 1996). Dyslexia is 'a controversial term' (Ashman and Elkins 1998, p. 525) and there is certainly no clear-cut line separating dyslexics from all other individuals who do not read well (Høien & Lundberg 2000). Most, if not all, of the problems found in dyslexic children are also found in the so-called 'garden variety' poor readers (McCoy 1995; Prior 1996; Siegel 1998). The obvious need for effective teaching to help them overcome their difficulties is equally strong in both groups.

In terms of pedagogy, it is difficult to visualise any teaching method found to be helpful to children diagnosed as dyslexic that would not also be highly relevant for other children with 'non-dyslexic' literacy learning problems. If one examines the literature on teaching methodology for remediation of dyslexia (for example, Birsch 1999; Miles 1983; Ott 1997; Thompson & Watkins 1990), one usually finds not a unique reading methodology applicable only to dyslexic children, but a range of teaching strategies that would be helpful to all children. Possible exceptions to this rule would be the more controversial therapeutic approaches such as diet control, perceptual-motor training, use of the Irlen tinted lenses and the various approaches to 'neurological re-programming'. The value of most of these approaches is still being seriously questioned (Spafford & Grosser 1996).

So where does this leave us? McCoy (1995) says that dyslexia is a non-specific concept of little value, and Prior (1996, p. 162) notes that:

> Reading disability is neither a disease nor a psychiatric disorder, and there
> is a reasonable case for considering it the lower part of a continuum of reading
> capacity with no established pathological implications.

Similarly, Allington and Baker (1999) suggest that children who find learning to read and write difficult are best served by designing and delivering sufficient and appropriate instruction rather than by identifying them with some label. Birsh (1999, p. xix), drawing on evidence from the best available research information, describes such appropriate instruction as 'highly systematic, structured, explicit and intensively multi-sensory'.

# 4 General teaching approaches

A reading program should be good enough to make every child competent.
(McGuinness 1998, p. 186)

There are two main approaches to reading instruction, the 'meaning–emphasis' approach and the 'skills-based' or 'code–emphasis' approach (Marzano & Paynter 1994). Each approach represents different beliefs about the processes involved in reading and the way in which children acquire reading skills.

Within the two broad approaches several different teaching methods exist. At different periods of time particular teaching methods or materials have been popular for a while, only to fall out of favour. Enthusiasm has been shown in the past for the phonic-word method, initial teaching alphabet, words in colour, look-and-say method, whole-word method, linguistic reading, language-experience approach, organic reading, literature-based reading and the whole language approach. In practice, teachers usually claim to use a combination of methods, rather than adhering rigidly to only one. The main point on which teachers tend to differ significantly is the extent to which they believe phonic skills should be taught directly and systematically, rather than acquired informally.

The meaning–emphasis approach is based on a belief that readers do not operate most of the time at the level of decoding print, but rather at the level of building meaning by identifying a few important words and using the minimum number of cues necessary in the text to guess or predict the information on the page. It is believed that children will acquire the component skills and strategies necessary for effective reading and writing mainly through incidental learning. This perspective was discussed briefly in Chapter 2.

In contrast to the meaning–emphasis approach, the skills-based approach is founded on the belief that a learner needs to be taught explicitly the component skills and strategies necessary for processing print. These skills include phonemic awareness, letter recognition, all levels of phonic decoding, sound blending, sight recognition of words and the identification of unfamiliar words by analogy with known words. Strategies required include those needed for comprehending and learning from text, such as self-questioning while reading, self-monitoring, self-correction to restore meaning, identifying and summarising main ideas, predicting, inferring and evaluating critically what is read.

Each approach has much to offer but also some shortcomings if used exclusively. Later it will be argued that the trend towards a 'balanced approach', combining the best of skills-based and meaning–emphasis principles, is likely to produce the optimum results for the greatest number of children. The evidence suggests that the principles of whole language teaching, plus explicit instruction in decoding skills and comprehension strategies, represent the most thorough approach to literacy teaching (Pressley 1998). This view is becoming widely accepted by teachers.

## Meaning–emphasis approaches

Meaning–emphasis approaches include such methods as 'shared book experience', 'guided reading', 'literature-based reading' and 'language-experience approach' – all of which can be subsumed under the title 'whole language'. The philosophy of whole language emphasises purposeful reading and writing at all times. Its advocates are critical of any approach that seeks to develop specific skills at the possible expense of the authenticity of the learning situation (Goodman 1989; Marzano & Paynter 1994; Tilstone *et al.* 2000). Whole language teachers are critical of teaching methods that break learning down into steps. They favour a less structured and more open-ended approach, with children immersed in interesting language-rich topics rather than in formal teacher-directed lessons. In particular, they are very much against contrived and decontextualised worksheet exercises designed to drill and practise certain language skills in isolation.

Whole language theory holds that learning to read is a natural process (Cambourne 1988; Riley 1999), much like learning to listen and speak, and for this reason it does not need to be broken down into separate skills and concepts and directly taught. The approach itself is often termed 'holistic', with children 'learning to read by reading' rather than putting together component skills (Goodman 1989). Whole language theory holds that authentic literacy experiences foster a child's understanding of the true nature and purposes of reading whereas the teaching of component skills may fail to achieve this goal.

At classroom level, the implementation of the whole language approach usually embodies the following teaching strategies:

- reading good literature to children every day and having 'real' literature available for children to read for themselves;
- providing time each day for shared reading;
- discussing and reflecting upon stories or other texts;
- encouraging silent reading;
- providing daily opportunities for children to read and write for real purposes;
- encouraging children to invent the spelling for words they do not know;
- adopting a conference-process approach to writing (drafting, sharing, editing and revising with feedback from teacher and peers);

- assisting children with any particular aspect of reading and writing at the time they require such guidance (the 'teachable moment');

- teaching specific skills always within the context of material being read or written;

- integrating language and literacy activities across all areas of the curriculum.

## What are the strengths in whole language?

Pressley (1998) reviews a number of studies evaluating the effectiveness of the whole language approach – especially those of Dahl and Freppon (1995) and Stahl, McKenna and Pagnucco (1994). He concludes that when whole language practices are skilfully implemented, they can:

- benefit children in the earliest stages of learning to read;

- increase children's awareness of the purposes and processes of reading and writing;

- build positive attitudes towards books and writing;

- help children develop strategies for interpreting text beyond the literal level (for example, prediction, inference, critical reading, reflection);

- enrich children's vocabulary and general knowledge;

- encourage risk-taking with invented spelling.

With these positive features in mind, it is clear that the whole language approach makes a major contribution to children's overall progress towards literacy. The question remains, however, whether whole language practice is comprehensive and intensive enough to ensure that all children become knowledgeable and competent in every aspect of reading, writing and spelling.

## Does the whole language approach suit all children?

Whole language may not suit the learning characteristics of all children. As mentioned in Chapter 3 teaching approaches lacking clear direction and structure can cause difficulties for some learners. The study by Stahl and Miller (1989) suggests that while the approach produced encouraging results with the most able children, positive whole language effects were much less likely in weaker children and in those children disadvantaged by a low socio-economic background. This finding is not surprising as many studies have shown that readers with learning difficulties, or with a socio-cultural disadvantage, tend to need highly systematic, direct and intensive instruction that matches their developmental level. Birsh (1999, p. xix) observes:

> Whole language instruction used in isolation has been found to be counterproductive with children with learning disabilities or children at risk of not learning to read; and has been found to produce fewer gains in word recognition and decoding skills than does instruction based on phonics.

### What are the weaknesses in whole language?

The whole language approach is often criticised because its holistic framework tends to underrate the importance of skill development, particularly the explicit teaching of the alphabetic principle and phonic decoding skills. Chall (1995) refers to the disappointing results for some children when reading teaching is based only on meaning emphasis and not on phonics. Marzano and Paynter (1994) caution that without skill development to a level of automaticity, complex processes like reading comprehension and writing cannot be performed efficiently.

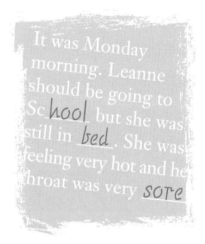

Whole language enthusiasts often fail to acknowledge that some children do not discover the alphabetic principle on their own, are not skilled in using contextual cues and therefore need systematic direct instruction (Castle 1999; Share & Stanovich 1995).

Tunmer and Chapman (1999) point out that the use of 'real books' rather than graded texts can be particularly problematic with beginning readers and older children with reading difficulties. The fact that so many of the words encountered in 'real' literature are used infrequently means that the student has to expend much time and effort in initially identifying them but then does not see them again often enough to store them as sight words. Difficult text may force the children to rely too much on guessing as their main word identification strategy.

Share and Stanovich (1995) point out the following weaknesses in the whole language approach:

- The efficacy of contextual guessing is overestimated.

- Reading acquisition is not like oral language acquisition; it is not acquired 'naturally' and needs to be taught.

- Early reading is not exactly the same as mature reading and therefore a single stage, meaning emphasis, top-down model is inadequate to describe it.

- Insistence on always learning skills in context can be unnecessarily limiting. Sometimes studying a skill or concept out of context can help the learner to focus more easily on salient aspects.

## Skills-based approaches to reading instruction

Probably no teacher ever uses a skill-based approach *exclusively*. To do so would be to teach reading and writing in the most unnatural way, working from parts to whole and only engaging in meaningful reading once all the skills were in place. What teachers who favour explicit teaching of skills do, however, is embed this instruction appropriately within their total literacy programme. Due attention is given to developing and applying skills for decoding, spelling and comprehending text.

Within what is termed the skills-based approach to reading there are at least three methods available to facilitate the teaching of decoding skills. These are referred to as synthetic phonics, analytic phonics and analogic phonics. Research strongly supports the value of teaching phonic knowledge and skills by any of these methods. There is no evidence that any one method is superior (Cunningham 2000; Strickland 2000). In practice, a thorough treatment of phonic skills within the reading curriculum should involve children in experience with all three ways of working with letter–sound relationships.

Under an extreme form of the skills approach (for example, Englemann, Haddox & Bruner 1983) phonic decoding is taught directly, using a highly structured format that begins with single letter-to-sound correspondences and gradually progresses to larger letter groups. At each stage, knowledge of basic letter-to-sound correspondences is applied to word-building and sound-blending. Phonic knowledge is also used to decode and encode words when reading meaningful text and when writing. This approach, beginning with sounds and letters and moving on to word-building and decoding, is often termed *synthetic phonics*. To be successful with synthetic phonics the learner must have good auditory discrimination, efficient sound-blending skill and the ability to store and retrieve easily basic sound–symbol relationships from long-term memory. For some children with learning difficulties these prerequisites are not always fully developed. This weakness almost certainly contributes to their reading problem.

A different approach to phonics instruction, but one still aiming to establish basic knowledge of letter-to-sound correspondences, involves commencing with a few words the children know by sight and breaking these words down to identify their component sounds and the letters representing these sounds (*analytic phonics*). It is sometimes argued that an analytic approach has advantages over the synthetic approach in that it begins with meaningful units (words) rather than with meaningless units (phonemes and letters). Most teachers using a phonic approach combine both synthetic and analytic activities in the reading curriculum they provide. Children do need to learn how to break words down into phonic units and how to combine phonic units to make words; these complementary processes are basic to both reading and spelling. To be successful with analytic phonics a learner needs to have good auditory discrimination, good phonemic segmentation skills and the ability to store and retrieve easily basic sound–symbol relationships from long-term memory. Again, these prerequisite skills present areas of weakness in some children with learning difficulties.

A third variant of the skills-based approach is often combined with either of the two above approaches, particularly once children have mastered the simplest level of letter–sound knowledge. This approach teaches children to recognise spelling patterns (for example, rimes, syllables) shared by a number of different words (*analogic phonics*). Given that skilled reading appears to rely heavily on swift recognition of such spelling patterns within words, teaching analogic phonic skills would seem to have merit, provided that the children can apply what they learn to reading connected text with increased fluency. To be successful with analogic phonics the learner needs to have all the underlying prerequisite skills described above for synthetic and analytic phonics, together with adequate visual–sequential memory span to process, store and retrieve relevant orthographic patterns. Dyslexic children in particular present with weaknesses in these underlying abilities and this almost certainly contributes to their learning problem.

## Supplementary materials in a skills-based approach

Any skills-based approach usually requires a high degree of teacher direction using explicit instruction and a carefully sequenced curriculum (Spafford & Grosser 1996). In the past this structure has often been achieved through the use of some form of graded reading materials ('basal readers') in which particular skills and strategies were introduced and taught in sequential order. The reading books were usually written with a carefully controlled vocabulary and limited sentence length in order to achieve necessary repetition of key words and to facilitate practice in phonic decoding. Sometimes the materials in the reading program included supplementary teaching aids such as games, flashcards, worksheets and activities to facilitate practice in word recognition, word-building and spelling.

Skills-based books and materials have been severely criticised by whole language exponents because the books tend to use rather trivial stories and present an unnatural style of language (Weaver 2000). It is suggested that these graded reading books can be detrimental to children's fluency, interest and motivation (Hoffman & McCarthey 2000). The books may cause children to believe that reading is only about sounding out words, not about making meaning and using context. It is also argued that although such books do enable children to apply and practise what they have been taught about letter–sound correspondences and word-building, the language patterns used in the early books are so stilted and unnatural that syntactic and semantic cues cannot be used (Teale & Yokota 2000). As a result of these criticisms, the use of graded reading books declined significantly in many countries during the 1980s and 1990s. There are, however, different viewpoints emerging now on the possible value of vocabulary-controlled reading books. Both Rubin (2000) and Pressley (1998) say that books with a high proportion of decodable words can be useful at a particular stage of a child's reading development. Easy decoding of text in the early stages of learning to read facilitates the automation of the decoding process and builds the reader's confidence in the decoding strategy.

## Potential weaknesses in the skills-based approach

Criticisms of the skills-based approach include:
* there is a danger that children engage in too many boring drill and practice activities and so fail to enjoy reading;

- rote learning may be used as a way of learning phonic relationships;
- skills taught out of context do not easily generalise and transfer to reading authentic text;
- when learning letter-to-sound correspondences children work with meaningless units, far removed from the real task of reading text to obtain meaning;
- learning abstract and arbitrary links between phonemes and letter symbols is not compatible with the cognitive ability of children aged 5 to 6 years;
- too many words in the English language are not 'regular' in their letter-to-sound correspondences and therefore phonic decoding often does not work;
- learning phonics actually makes reading more difficult.

The final three criticisms listed above are incorrect and based on false assumptions or wrong information. The first four criticisms have some truth in them and do need to be taken into account by teachers. It is sometimes said that in classrooms where a skills-based approach is used, children may spend more time doing routine exercises and practice sheets than actually reading books for information and enjoyment (Salinger 1993). This is unlikely to be true but it does highlight the need for teachers to realise that skills are not in themselves relevant end-points; they are only useful if they facilitate reading for meaning.

It is important to emphasise that teachers rarely deal with phonic skills in a totally decontextualised way. The vast majority of teachers who consider phonic skills to be essential for independence in reading and spelling simply embed the systematic teaching of phonics within their meaningful language arts program. They teach phonics through word-study activities, word families, spelling, writing and reading. They also check regularly to ensure that children are learning and applying the phonic skills needed when reading connected text and when writing for real purposes.

Regardless of the criticisms, skills-based approaches have fared very well indeed in studies designed to assess their effectiveness (for example, Adams 1990; Chall 1967) and have enjoyed something of a resurgence in popularity (Pressley 1998; Stuart *et al.* 1999). Osborn and Lehr (1998, p. 339) conclude that:

> The systematic and explicit instruction in decoding and comprehension skills has been neglected in recent years [but] the evidence that skills instruction is necessary is overwhelming. Particularly problematic is that many children do not acquire word recognition skills merely as a by-product of immersion in reading and writing … what is supported by evidence is that systematic and intensive decoding instruction provides an excellent start toward becoming a fluent reader.

## Swings of the phonics pendulum

Cunningham (1999) points out that in the second half of the twentieth century educators' views on the relative contribution of phonic skills to reading and spelling changed, not once but several times. Swings in popularity occurred roughly every decade from the 1950s. The early 1970s saw a return to skill-based instruction after a period of the whole-word recognition method. The change was due in part to the influence of Jeanne Chall's (1967) seminal study indicating that early systematic teaching of phonics produced significant advantages over other approaches in which phonic skills were not given high priority (for example, whole-word or meaning–emphasis method). The advantages were evident in terms of word recognition, vocabulary, comprehension and spelling for children in the beginning stages of reading.

By the end of that decade, the influence of the psycholinguistic school of thought caused a very strong reaction against the skills approach. Direct phonic instruction was again 'out'. The 1980s and early 1990s was the era of the whole language (meaning–emphasis) approach. In whole language teaching, phonic skills were given very low priority in the belief that children will learn all they need to know about letter–sound correspondences and decoding simply by engaging in daily reading and writing activities.

The 1990s saw another slow swing back in favour of phonics instruction as an essential part of a balanced approach to literacy teaching, mainly due to a better understanding of how readers actually process print, together with the hard evidence from research showing that all children need to be skilled in rapid decoding to become proficient and independent readers (Adams 1990).

The swings of this particular education pendulum were not entirely due to faddism and idiosyncratic variation in the popularity of different teaching methods. The changes reflected the beliefs held at particular times concerning how best to help students acquire reading and writing skills. The fact that different groups of educators have held very different beliefs is what turned the original 'great debate' concerning the best approach to reading instruction (Chall 1967) into the 'reading wars' of the late 1990s (Rasinski & Padak 1998; Reutzel 1999). Out of the debris of the reading wars, however, a clearer road for the future seems to be emerging.

## The current position on the teaching of phonics

In 1997 the influential International Reading Association (IRA) issued an important *Position Statement on the Role of Phonics in Reading Instruction*. In it the IRA fully supports the explicit teaching of phonic knowledge and skills in the early stages of reading instruction and recommends that such instruction must, if it is to generalise and be effective, be embedded in the meaningful context of reading and writing. Phonics instruction should not be provided in the form of totally decontextualised drill exercises. The typical worksheets purporting to provide practice in simple phonics are of limited value in helping children develop functional phonic skills for identifying words in books and for spelling the words they need as they write.

> When phonics instruction is linked to children's reading and writing, they are more likely to become strategic and independent in their use of phonics than when phonics instruction is drilled and practised in isolation. (IRA, 1997, p. 2)

The principles espoused by the IRA have been translated into operational terms by Hoffman and McCarthey (2000). They recommend that the teaching of phonics should be:

- *explicit* – not left to incidental learning;
- *pervasive* – made a teaching point within many different contextualised reading and writing activities;
- *systematic* – building from simple phonic skills to more complex letter clusters;
- *strategic* – showing when and how the use of phonic decoding is relevant and helpful;
- *diagnostic* – revealing what children already know, almost know, and what still remains to be taught.

Current beliefs are that specific reading skills, including phonic decoding, should be taught early and thoroughly, both within and alongside reading for meaning and enjoyment. These beliefs are likely to guide reading instruction during the twenty-first century.

## A balanced approach

It is recognised now that meaning–emphasis approaches and skills-based teaching both have very important contributions to make in fostering children's literacy development. There have been many calls for the adoption of a 'balanced approach' to literacy teaching that combines the best features of the two approaches described above (Freppon & Dahl 1998; Hoffman, Baumann & Afflerbach 2000; McIntyre & Pressley 1996; Pressley 1998; Reutzel 1999; Riley 1999; Searfoss, Readence & Mallette 2001). As Cunningham *et al.* (2000) indicate, children *need* a balanced literacy program if they are to develop all necessary skills and strategies for independence in reading and writing.

The notion of 'balance' within the literacy curriculum applies not only to *what* is taught (skills, concepts, strategies) but also to *how* it is taught (through explicit instruction, child-centred discovery, guided practice, structured materials). In the early stages of learning to read, the best curricula offer a balance of elements including reading for meaning, experience with high-quality literature, systematic instruction in phonics, development of sight vocabulary, and ample opportunities to read and write (Burns, Griffin & Snow 1999). Balance also involves the optimum mix of structured versus unstructured use of learning time, of ungraded versus graded teaching materials, of student choice versus teacher choice of themes, topics and resources, of individualised versus group programming (Blair-Larsen & Williams 1999).

A well-balanced literacy programme is not achieved, however, simply by creating a random eclectic combination of various instructional approaches and resources. McGuinness (1998) speaks very strongly against the notion that a balanced reading programme means throwing in a little bit of everything – some look-and-say, a little phonics, exposure to real books, and so forth. A balanced approach requires a very thoughtful selection of appropriate teaching techniques and content to assist children who are at particular stages of literacy development (Searfoss *et al.* 2001). The balance of elements may need to change significantly as the beginning reader gradually becomes a more competent reader. For example, initial heavy emphasis on phonic skills and decoding could give way to extended practice in the application of reading comprehension strategies. The balance of elements in the programme may also need to be adjusted if a child is not making optimum progress.

Within a balanced reading programme Spiegel (1999) argues convincingly for a blend of explicit instruction and child-centred learning adjusted as far as possible to the needs of individual children and to the demands of the particular learning activity. She provides guidelines to help a teacher decide on the emphasis (balance) to be given at any particular time in the programme. The summary below is adapted from Spiegel (1999, pp. 250–1).

When considering the learner, a teacher should move more towards teacher-directed instruction if the child:

- falls behind peers as a result of too little teacher direction;
- runs the risk of a cumulative difficulty because he or she never quite learns what the other children are learning;
- is losing confidence and interest when trying to work independently.

A teacher should move more towards learner-directed instruction if a child:

- has been able to learn effective strategies primarily through his or her own explorations;
- will be held back and lose interest by having to listen to suggestions for accomplishing a task he or she already knows how to do.

When considering the learning task, a teacher should move more towards teacher-directed explicit instruction if an essential strategy, skill or concept is being taught for the first time.

A teacher should move more towards learner-centred instruction if:

- the concept or strategy can be easily learned through children's own exploration;
- the concept does not provide a foundation for other concepts and therefore does not need to be learned at a particular time.

In terms of curricular balance, Hoffman and McCarthey (2000) recommend the following basic principles to ensure that a literacy programme teaches children all they need to learn.

- Make sure that word recognition skills are thoroughly developed – this involves explicit teaching of the alphabetic principle, phonic decoding skills and the effective use of contextual cueing systems. The balance will shift over time from much direct teaching and close monitoring in the early stages to much more independent and self-regulated application by the child.
- Use texts that are structured to teach as well as those that have narrative – at the earliest levels of reading development this may mean using some books with controlled vocabulary and a high proportion of decodable words. Books with predictable and repetitive language patterns are also particularly useful. At the higher levels of reading proficiency, this means using text books effectively as a medium to cover core information in particular subject areas; for example, science, environmental education and geography.
- Ensure that the child engages in ample successful reading practice using meaningful texts – sustained and intensive practice is the single most important ingredient in helping all children improve their reading fluency and confidence (Berger, Henderson & Morris 1999). There is a positive correlation between children's reading competency and the time they spend reading connected text. If young children spend at least fifteen minutes a day reading, it makes a significant difference in their reading ability (Teale & Yokota 2000). Practice should involve mainly the use of texts at the child's independent reading level (very low error rate). Practice with difficult text will not improve fluency and will undermine confidence and motivation.
- Teach and encourage the use of strategic reading behaviours – this type of teaching usually requires the teacher in the first instance to demonstrate specific strategies: how to identify difficult words, find the main idea in a passage of text, summarise main points, monitor one's own level of understanding. (See Chapters 5 and 6 for additional suggestions.)
- Use reading as a means of extending knowledge ('reading to learn') – from the earliest stages of reading development children should use books to discover new information, raise questions and solve problems.

- Encourage reading for pleasure and reflection – this extremely important goal must be given high priority. It will often be the most difficult goal to achieve with children who have reading difficulties and who have experienced little satisfaction from struggling with text. The challenge for the teacher and the parent is to try to find books that really appeal to these children, and then to equip them with the necessary skills to become more competent and confident.

# 5 Specific teaching methods and strategies

Reading is something that has to be taught and learned. (Høien & Lundberg 2000, p. 14)

The methods and strategies described in this chapter for developing beginning, intermediate and more advanced reading skills enable teachers to combine principles from whole language philosophy with appropriate amounts of skills-based instruction within an integrated and balanced approach to reading.

## Methods and strategies

The methods and strategies outlined below can be used very flexibly with a whole class or a group of children. They can also be adapted easily and applied in a more structured way when tutoring individual children who have learning difficulties. In all cases the teaching of reading is encouraged as a thinking process, with an emphasis on understanding.

### Shared book experience

The teaching method known as shared book experience (SBE) owes much to the influence of Don Holdaway (1982; 1990), a New Zealand educator. The strategy has obvious application with young children in the first year of schooling but the principles can also be applied to older children with learning difficulties if age-appropriate and appealing books are used. It is an excellent method for establishing the beginnings of reading.

The theory underpinning SBE derives from whole language philosophy and is based on the belief that learning to read is a social experience and that children can learn through positive guidance and support via the medium of group reading experiences (Rasinski & Padak 2000). The principles still apply even if the 'group' comprises one supportive adult and the child who is being assisted.

SBE aims to develop children's:

- enjoyment and interest in books;
- concepts about print;
- phonemic awareness;
- awareness of syntactical patterns;
- use of contextual cues;

- word recognition skills;
- phonic knowledge;
- comprehension strategies.

The basic principles and strategies of SBE have become widely accepted as valuable for building on the understandings developed during the emergent literacy stage. For example, SBE encourages children to interact positively with books and develop a love of stories, songs and rhymes, reinforces concepts about print, and begins the process of talking about and reflecting upon what is read (Fisher & Medvic 2000). The approach also encourages co-operative learning and sharing in a small group situation or between an adult and a child. The method can provide a valuable compensatory purpose for children who enter school lacking rich language and literacy experiences from the preschool years.

In SBE, children have stories read to them by the teacher or parent using a large-size, well-illustrated book with print big enough to be seen easily by the children. After discussing the cover picture, the title and perhaps some of the illustrations within the book, the teacher asks the children to say what they think the story will be about. The teacher then reads the story to the group in a lively and interesting manner, using good expression and normal fluency to hold the children's attention. After the reading the teacher invites comments from the children and asks them questions about the story and the characters in it. The questions are not restricted simply to the literal (factual) level but may also encourage prediction, interpretation, reflection and criticism.

The first reading of the story is usually completed without interruption. The aim is to enjoy and discuss the story. After the discussion and questioning, the story is read again. This time the children are encouraged to join in with some of the reading, particularly with repetitive parts of the text (for example, 'Not I', said the cat. 'Not I', said the dog. 'Not I', said the pig'.) Children's attention may be directed to certain words on the page, and in later readings, to particular spelling patterns shared by some words. The pages of the book become a giant teaching-aid on which the teacher can develop word recognition, decoding skills and use of context. The teacher may, for example, cover a word on the page and ask the children to predict what the word is from the meaning and structure of the sentence. By covering only the final part of the word the children would be encouraged to use initial letter cue to aid prediction. At a later stage some of the same learning experiences can be extended to cloze passage activity (see *cloze procedure* p. 57). The teacher may draw the children's attention to the same word (for example, dragon) in different places on the page. The children can find other words on the page beginning with 'dr'. They can break the word into two words 'drag' and 'on'. If appropriate, they can work at the blackboard later and make other words from 'drag'; for example, bag, lag, tag, sag, gag, nag, rag, wag, flag, brag, snag – beginning to lay the foundation for orthographic pattern recognition.

Most SBE sessions also involve the children in some writing and drawing associated with the material from the big book.

It should be noted that SBE, when skilfully implemented, embodies all the basic principles of effective teaching, particularly the important elements of attention-holding, demonstration, modelling, active participation and successful practice. The approach is also soundly based upon, and replicates, some aspects of 'bedtime stories' read to children at home during the emergent literacy stage. Many of the subtle teaching interactions that occur during shared reading (for example, reflecting, questioning, word identification) can and should be taught to parents for use with their own children at home or to tutors working with problem readers. Klesius and Griffith (1998) summarise the main behaviours of the teacher during shared reading as:

- motivating
- demonstrating
- developing story structure
- questioning
- clarifying information
- extending vocabulary
- drawing attention to key features of pictures or text
- scaffolding children's thinking
- praising
- extending children's responses
- summarising.

Teachers using SBE need to prepare well for the lesson so that the reading, questioning and discussions all move smoothly and with purpose, and to ensure that opportunities are not missed to teach word recognition, phonic knowledge and use of context – although this must never dominate the lesson. Selection of suitable books is also very important. Ideal books are those with predictable language patterns, some degree of repetition of words within the story and a limited amount of print on each page. Some published 'big books' also have conventional-size books containing the same pictures and words so that children can practise the reading individually or with a partner at school and at home.

The great strength of SBE lies in the fact that it allows very important knowledge, skills and strategies to be taught and learned entirely through the medium of authentic reading experiences. Sharing books and stories in this way is of value to all children, including those with reading difficulties (Gunning 2001; Klesius & Griffith 1998; Searfoss, Readence & Mallette 2001; Snow, Burns & Griffin 1998). It is a strategy that enables children to participate fully or partially in a meaningful language and print activity even before they can recognise many words or associate letters with sounds (Fountas & Pinnell 1999). The way in which skilled teachers manage to hold the attention and interest of the group of children during SBE is an excellent illustration of establishing what is known as 'engaged reading'. When readers are fully engaged in a task, they are active participants and gain some degree of self-regulation and independence. Engagement of this type is known to increase learning (Mosenthal 1999), but it can be extremely difficult to establish such engagement in children who have already had many learning failures. SBE provides an opportunity to restore confidence and to begin to build a new foundation.

Teachers seeking more information on SBE should consult Holdaway (1990), Klesius and Griffith (1998), or Fisher and Medvic (2000). Brief descriptions will also be found in most reading and remedial reading methodology texts (for example, Cunningham *et al.* 2000; Gunning 2001; Rasinski & Padak 2000; Searfoss, Readence & Mallette 2001; Walker 2000; Westwood 1997).

The SBE approach links very effectively with the language-experience approach (LEA) and guided reading (GR). All three approaches allow implementation of the principle of 'balanced' attention to meaning, motivation and skill development. The use of any of these approaches enables a teacher to integrate whole language philosophy with explicit teaching of appropriate skills.

## Language-experience approach

The language-experience approach (LEA) is sometimes known as 'dictated story approach' (Taylor *et al.* 1996) and this description does capture the main feature of the method. The principles of LEA are summed up in the following statements:

What I know about, I can talk about.

What I say can be written down by someone.

I can read what has been written.

The child being taught using LEA talks about a chosen topic related to his or her own knowledge and experience. What the child says is written down by a scribe (teacher, tutor, parent or peer). For example, he or she might talk about visiting a family member, watching a favourite cartoon on television or playing with friends. An adult with literacy problems using LEA in a tutorial setting may talk about his or her family, work, sports, holidays, leisure or other interests. What is written becomes the vocabulary and the sentence structures used to help the child acquire word recognition strategies and the beginnings of phonic skills.

Nessel and Jones (1981, p. 1) describe LEA thus:

The language-experience approach is a means of teaching children to read by capitalizing on their interests, experiences and oral language facility. Children dictate stories and accounts based on their experiences; these materials are then used as the basis of the reading program.

This 'writing approach to reading' is actually very flexible and can be adapted to meet the needs of a wide range of learners (Vacca, Vacca & Gove 2000). LEA has proved to be a very effective teaching approach for beginning readers, for children of any age who have significant learning difficulties and for adults with literacy problems. It is also highly appropriate for children with intellectual disability in special schools (Westwood 1994) and for children with English as a second language (Gunning 2000). When used for remedial purposes, it is usually implemented individually but it can also be carried out with groups of children after discussion of some common experience they have all shared (Gunning 2000; Rubin 2000).

From the viewpoint of teaching children with learning problems, LEA has two great advantages over the use of published books. There is the opportunity to utilise the child's own interests to generate material for reading, writing and discussion, and the teacher is able to work at all times within the child's current level of language competence.

The child's main resource for this approach is the language-experience book into which each of his or her dictated messages, stories, letters or reports are written. The book provided for the beginning stages is typically the size of a scrapbook (larger than A4 size). On each page there will be some writing and a picture, either drawn by the child or cut from a newspaper or magazine and pasted on the page. For the beginner there may be no more that a few words below the picture. Use of the 'personal photograph' book has been used very successfully as a starting point for children with intellectual disability or communication difficulties (Berger, Henderson & Morris 1999).

## A structured use of the language-experience approach

On day 1, for a child with severe reading difficulties functioning at beginner level, the teacher or tutor might write:

### This is a photo of me.

The child watches as the adult 'scribe' writes the dictated statement.

The adult reads what is written to the child. Then they read it twice together with the child pointing to each word.

The child copies the sentence below the teacher's writing.

The adult may say, 'Put your finger on the word *photo*. Good! Look at the word *me*. Close your eyes and try to imagine the word *me*. Now see if you can write *me* on this page. Good! See if you can write *photo*'.

The sentence is written again on a strip of paper and cut into separate words.

The child rearranges the words to make the sentence.

The teacher picks up the words, shuffles them and uses them as flashcards to practise word recognition with the child.

The child assembles the words again in the correct order.

The child writes the words without help (and if possible from memory) in a vocabulary list at the back of the language experience book.

Next day the child is helped to write:

My name is Stephen.

I am 14.

The same procedure described above is followed in order to learn this new material.

At least twice a week the child reads the recordings from the previous lessons.

The words in the vocabulary list are also revised frequently, both in terms of sight recognition and spelling.

Some weeks later the child might be writing (and reading fluently):

I go into town with my friend.

Sometimes we buy a video.

We buy drinks at the shop near the train station.

It costs £2 on the train to get home.

Next week we may go to see a film.

As well as daily reading and writing, the child must soon be taught some basic phonic knowledge so that he or she will be able to decode unfamiliar words and begin to spell some of the words needed in the daily writing. Often the phonics work can be based on a word or words taken from the writing for that day and designed to develop orthographic awareness of letter patterns:

| friend | end |
| bend | send |
| mend | lend |

Extracting words and phonic units from the language-experience recordings alone will not be sufficiently systematic to ensure that the child acquires an adequate grounding in sight vocabulary or phonic knowledge. It is usual to supplement this experience by spending a little time each lesson in direct teaching of word-attack skills, decoding and spelling based on appropriate vocabulary lists. (See Chapter 6 for content and methods for phonics and word study.)

As the child begins to gain reading skills and strategies from the LEA materials and the supplementary work, it is valuable to select carefully a published book that he or she can also begin to read. By carefully inspecting the chosen book, the teacher can identify important and difficult vocabulary so that this can be pre-taught before the book is introduced to the child. Pre-teaching the vocabulary will increase the chances of success when the child first attempts to read the text.

As time goes by, the amount written each day by the child will increase, while the amount of direct help given by the adult can decrease. The scrapbook format gives way to an exercise book or loose-leaf file. By this time, the child is also being helped to read conventional books at an appropriate level of difficulty.

The language-experience approach will fail as a remedial intervention method if:

- Too much material is written each day and the child cannot retain the words in the long-term memory. Controlling the amount written each day is the responsibility of the teacher or tutor.

- Too little time is spent in practising word recognition. Abundant repetition and overlearning is the only way to ensure that the words taken from the LEA recordings are converted to sight vocabulary and automatically recognised in and out of context.

- The child does not also receive systematic instruction in phonics and spelling.

It is expected that the LEA sessions will occur for about 15 to 20 minutes *daily*. If the child receives help in reading only once or twice a week it is extremely difficult to create and maintain the same level of success and continuity. This is true, of course, of any teaching approach used for remedial purposes.

Teachers wishing to find out more information about LEA can read Walker (2000, pp. 247–9) or Cunningham *et al.* (2000, pp. 41–8). The book by Stauffer (1980) *The Language-Experience Approach to the Teaching of Reading* provides the most detailed coverage available.

A useful activity that can be used to complement learning experiences from SBE and LEA is *cloze procedure*.

## Cloze procedure

Activities using 'cloze procedure' are often useful in encouraging the use of contextual cues and to ensure that the reader is using meaning to predict words in a passage (Ott 1997). Cloze procedure usually involves the deletion of certain words, or parts of words, in the printed passage, leaving spaces of uniform size. The reader is required to read the passage and suggest an appropriate word to fill the space. For example:

> It was Monday morning. Leanne should be going to sch＿ but she was still in＿. She was feeling very hot and her throat was very＿.
>
> 'I think I should send for the＿', her mother said. 'No school for you＿'.
>
> Leanne turned over and went back to＿.

Variations on the cloze procedure involve leaving the initial letter or letters of the missing word to provide a clue; providing the word ending but not the beginning; giving multiple choice instead of deleting the word; deleting two or more consecutive words.

Cloze activities can be used as exercises in their own right with individual children or as follow-up to a shared book, language experience or guided reading lesson (Walker 2000). They can also be used with a group or class. In a group situation the children discuss all the possible alternative words and then reach consensus on the most appropriate word to fill the space. The children are using vocabulary, syntax, semantic and sometimes partial grapho-phonic cues to determine the best alternative.

## Guided reading

The 'guided reading' approach – also known as guided reading procedure (GRP) – is considered to be an essential part of any balanced approach to literacy (Blair-Larsen & Williams 1999). It addresses the need to help children become better comprehenders of text at various levels of sophistication, and better at processing and recalling important information from text. While the guidance provided may focus at times on specific skills such as word identification and decoding, or on vocabulary development, its main thrust is to assist with the development of a strategic approach to reading comprehension. Fountas and Pinnell (1996, p. 2) describe guided reading as, '… a context in which a teacher supports each reader's development of effective strategies for processing novel texts at increasingly challenging levels of difficulty'.

In the reading methodology literature, guided reading is most often suggested as an approach to use with children after the third or fourth year of schooling. It is presented as an excellent way of developing a strategic, reflective and critical approach in children who are beyond the beginner stage. Most of the suggestions for providing guidance are, however, merely extensions of what should have been occurring at earlier age levels during SBE and in discussions stemming from children's language-experience material.

There are three main stages at which guidance from the teacher is provided: *before* reading the text, *during* the reading and *after* the reading. To enable these processes to operate effectively, the learning environment needs to be supportive and encouraging.

## Before reading

Guidance before reading is in many ways similar to the 'advance organiser' activity typical of some textbooks or programmed materials. It prepares the reader to enter the text with some clear purpose and a plan of action in mind. At the 'before reading' stage the teacher may, for example, focus children's attention on any prior knowledge they have that relates to the topic, encourage them to generate questions or make predictions about information to be presented in the text, remind them of effective ways of reading the material, alert them to look out for certain points, or pre-teach some difficult vocabulary to be encountered later in the text.

## During reading

The guidance during reading may again encourage the children to generate questions, look for cause–effect relationships, compare and contrast information, react critically, check for understanding and highlight main ideas.

## After reading

The guidance after reading may help the children to summarise and retell, check for understanding and recall and encourage critical reflection and evaluation.

The guided reading sessions are usually conducted by the teacher but with heavy emphasis placed on children's active participation through discussion, co-operative learning and sharing of ideas (Searfoss, Readence & Mallette 2001). Guidance can also be provided – particularly for reasonably proficient readers and older children – in the form of printed 'study guides' (Marinak & Henk 1999).

The processes involved in guided reading sessions, while primarily serving a teaching function, also allow the teacher to observe and assess children's comprehension strategies (Fawson & Reutzel 2000). Fountas and Pinnell (1996) consider this to be a very important diagnostic function, enabling a teacher to adapt reading guidance to match children's specific needs and to ensure that all children are developing into more independent and critical readers over a period of time.

One of the best sources for additional information on guided reading is the text by Fountas and Pinnell (1996). A rich and valuable source of ideas and activities to use within the pre-reading, during reading and after-reading phases of the lesson are described by Yopp and Yopp (2001). Their book is highly recommended. The text by Vacca, Vacca and Gove (2000, pp. 275–80) contains some useful ideas under the general heading 'Guiding interactions between reader and text'. In that section the authors describe the directed reading–thinking activity (DRTA) and the KWL strategy. These two approaches to improving comprehension are summarised briefly below.

## Directed reading–thinking activity

Directed reading–thinking activity (DRTA) is an instructional strategy designed to give children experience in predicting what an author will say, reading the text to confirm or revise the predictions and elaborating upon responses (Walker 2000). Questioning by the teacher encourages children to think more analytically and critically about the subject matter they are reading (Rubin 2000).

The process involves the reader in three basic steps:

1   Predicting some of the information he or she may find or raising some questions he or she hopes to have answered in the text.

2   Reading the text carefully, with predictions and questions in mind.

3   Being able to prove, with evidence from the text, any conclusions made from the reading.

The teacher's involvement is mainly the asking of relevant focus questions to activate the children's thinking: What do you think will happen? What is this going to be about? How would she be feeling? Why do you think that? Can you prove what you say from something in the book?

The DRTA approach can be used with children at any stage of reading development. It is easily accommodated at a simple level in shared book sessions or at a level involving higher order thinking with older readers when they process more difficult text. In remedial contexts DRTA can be used to involve the reader more actively in thinking about what has been read after having struggled to decode the passage. In order for some children with reading difficulties to get the most benefit from DRTA it is usually necessary to have them re-read the passage, aiming for improved fluency so that cognitive effort can be redirected towards the meaning of the words.

## K–W–L strategy (Know. Want to know. Learned.)

The KWL strategy was created by Ogle (1986) and has subsequently been recommended in many reading methodology texts. One version of the strategy that can be used with a class, a small group or an individual involves the preparation of a 'KWL chart'. The chart is ruled up with three columns headed:

| What we know | What we want to know | What we learned |
|---|---|---|
|  |  |  |

Immediately before a non-fiction text is to be read, the children and teacher together brainstorm and write down all they know about the topic as dot-points under the first column (activating prior knowledge). Under the second column they generate some questions or issues they hope the text may answer (predicting, questioning and seeking information). After reading the text, either silently or as a shared activity, the children write in the third column a dot-point summary of the main things they have learned from the text (reflecting, consolidating, evaluating, summarising). If their questions in column two have been answered the information is noted, but the summary in the final column is not restricted simply to answering the predetermined questions.

A fourth column might be added to the chart in which children could record their own feelings about the material in the text or write down suggestions for what they will do next in order to make use of the information they have learned or to extend their study of the same topic (Yopp & Yopp 2001).

The KWL strategy can also be used with texts other than non-fiction but the teacher needs to select material that lends itself to this type of treatment.

It is vital that teachers themselves prepare carefully for lessons in which this type of activity is to occur. The teacher must have read the text thoroughly beforehand, have in mind suitable activities for the three stages (before reading, during reading and after reading), and have at hand any additional resource materials that may be required. The teacher must also keep in mind the purposes of the strategy; namely, to stimulate children's thinking about text and to provide an appropriate format for encouraging discussion, predicting, questioning, investigating, reflecting, thinking, evaluating and summarising.

Examples of the KWL strategy in use are provided in Vacca, Vacca & Gove (2000) and Yopp and Yopp (2001).

## The 3 H strategy (Here. Hidden. In my Head.)

The purpose of this strategy is to teach children where the answers to their questions can be found. An answer is either explicitly stated in the text (*here* on the page), implied in the text and can be deduced if the reader uses some information given on the page and combines it with prior knowledge (*hidden*), or not on the page but already in the child's background knowledge (in the learner's *head*). In teaching the 3 H strategy, the children are cued to use appropriate text-based or knowledge-based information to answer specific questions. They are also taught to use self-questioning to focus their own attention on selecting appropriate sources of information and to monitor their performance. Cue cards can be used initially as support.

Teaching of the strategy involves the following steps:

1   Teacher demonstration and 'thinking aloud' while applying the first step in the strategy (locating information *here* on the page).

2   Children practise applying this step, with feedback from the teacher.

3   Teacher demonstration and 'thinking aloud' for the second step (*hidden* information).

4   Children practise step 1 and step 2, with guidance and feedback.

5   Teacher demonstration of the third step (information is not *here* or *hidden* and has to be retrieved from a source outside the text).

6   Children practise step 1, step 2 and step 3 with guidance and feedback.

7   Strategy is used extensively on a variety of text types.

8   Teacher provides prompts and cues in the beginning but these are slowly withdrawn as children gain confidence and control of the strategy.

The 3 H strategy was adapted by Graham and Wong (1993) from a similar question-and-answer procedure devised by Raphael and Pearson (1985). Graham and Wong (1993) report evidence from a study of upper primary children showing that the 3 H strategy can improve reading comprehension and increase children's metacognitive functioning related to the comprehension task.

## PQRS reading strategy

The PQRS strategy is a simple, step-by-step plan of action any child might adopt when faced with a reading assignment (Westwood 1997). The steps are described below.

1   P = Preview

The child scans the chapter or page, attending to headings, subheadings, diagrams or figures. Gains a general impression of what the text is likely to cover. Asks him or herself, 'What do I know already about this subject?'

2   Q = Question

The child generates some questions in his or her mind. 'What do I expect to learn from this?', 'Will it tell me how much the item costs?', 'Will it give the answer to the next question on my homework sheet?', 'Will I need to read this part carefully, or can I skim it?'

3   R = Read

The child reads the page carefully for information. Re-reads any difficult sections. Asks, 'Were my questions answered?' 'Do I need to check this again?' 'Do I understand everything on the page?'

4   S = Summarise

The child briefly states in his or her own words the main points from the text or draws conclusions from what has been read.

The teacher models the application of the PQRS strategy, demonstrating how to focus on key points in the text, check for understanding, back-track to gain contextual cues and self-correct. This modelling helps children to internalise the steps in the procedure. 'Thinking aloud' demonstrates how to question, check, reflect and summarise. The children are then taken through several sessions of guided practice using appropriate texts until they are confident about using the strategy independently.

PQRS, together with the other strategies described above, can be taught and practised through an approach called *reciprocal teaching*.

## Reciprocal teaching (RT)

The reciprocal teaching approach involves the teacher and the children taking turns to read, question and interpret a text (Pressley & McCormick 1995). The teacher begins by modelling an appropriate range of strategies for actively processing and extracting relevant information from a passage of text. The teacher may demonstrate:

- thinking aloud
- self-questioning
- predicting
- checking

- skimming
- re-reading
- confirming
- clarifying
- evaluating
- criticising
- summarising.

Once the children become familiar with the strategies modelled by the teacher, they are encouraged to take turns using similar strategies themselves as the group moves on through the text. For example, a child may ask the group to think critically about certain points in the text, recall and summarise what has been covered so far or discuss their attitude towards some idea presented by the author. The teacher's dominant role reduces and the children are now empowered to work co-operatively and actively with the material.

Reciprocal teaching in the domain of reading is most closely associated with the work of Palincsar and Brown (1984). The original version devised by Palinscar and Brown had just four elements: predicting, questioning, clarifying, and summarising. The approach is included here for two reasons: it is an effective way of developing strategic reading in children and the underlying principle of handing over control of strategies entirely to the learner is what any teacher, tutor or parent must attempt to do at appropriate stages in a remedial program. Too often children with learning difficulties remain passive during tutoring sessions dominated by the tutor, rather than taking the initiative themselves.

The research findings on RT are positive (Pressley & McCormick 1995; Rosenshine & Meister 1994) and in some studies the method has produced sizable gains in reading comprehension. It is not a particularly easy teaching method to use, particularly if the teacher does not work regularly with the group of children or does not have firm classroom control. The children need to have good rapport with the teacher and a supportive attitude to one another if the child-centred aspects of the lesson are to work productively. This is much less of a problem when RT is used with an individual or very small group in a remedial context. However, in both remedial and mainstream contexts the teacher needs to use the approach frequently enough to become competent and confident in its implementation and management (Vacca, Vacca & Gove 2000).

## Developing fluency

Fluency can be defined as 'the ability to read texts quickly and accurately' (Cooper 2000, p. 195). Fluency markedly influences a reader's ability to comprehend text, with slow reading seriously disrupting understanding. Carver (2000) places great emphasis on the need to help all readers develop fluency and suggests that this is one aspect of reading performance that is often neglected in the assessment of children and in terms of priority within intervention programmes.

The readability level of a book will, of course, have a great impact on reading fluency. If a text contains too many unfamiliar words the reader will struggle and become frustrated. The first step in attempting to increase fluency is to select a text at the correct readability level. For a book to be read easily by a child he or she should know at least 97 per cent of the words on the page. Texts with this rate of success are said to be at the child's independent reading level. If someone is available to help the child as he or she reads, then a text in which at least 90–95 per cent of the words are known can be used. This is termed the 'instructional level'. If the child knows less than 90 per cent of the words the book is deemed to be at 'frustration level'. Guppy and Hughes (1999), in a useful description of the levels of text difficulty and their effects, state that a poor reader should never be expected to read material at frustration level since this leads to a situation where the child ceases to expect to understand what he or she reads. They stress the importance of someone reading material at this more difficult level *to* the child in order to increase listening comprehension and to expose the child to new vocabulary in context and to more advanced sentence structures.

Assuming that the text is at an appropriate level of difficulty, Rasinski (1998) suggests that fluency can be improved by:

- reading the same passage several times;
- imitating the demonstration of a better reader;
- discussing the value and role of fluency with the child;
- training the reader to self-monitor and self-correct;
- pre-teaching any difficult vocabulary in the text.

## Repeated reading strategy

Repeated reading (RR) of a passage of text not only helps to improve fluency and comprehension but can also help convince a slower reader that, with practice, he or she can actually read material at the same rate, and with the same accuracy and expression, as other children. Most of the time poor readers hear themselves reading very slowly, tripping over too many words on the page and lacking any real expression. Spafford and Grosser (1996) give positive support to the frequent use of repeated reading to improve the fluency and confidence of children with reading difficulties. Re-reading text also allows children to automate and perfect the various skills and strategies they have been learning (Fowler 1998; Snow, Burns & Griffin 1998). It is unlikely that children will attain an automatic level of visual and orthographic decoding unless they encounter the same words frequently enough to store them in memory. Repeated reading makes this possible.

This writer has used repeated reading as a regular component in many remedial contexts, both at primary and secondary level. The procedure is for the teacher first to model clearly the reading aloud of a paragraph of about fifty words, while the child follows the print on the page. The teacher and child together then read the same paragraph. Finally, the child reads the paragraph unaided – twice or three times if necessary – aiming for improved accuracy, fluency and expression. At least once each week the child's oral reading of a practised passage is recorded on tape and played back. This provides clear evidence to the child that he or she is capable of fluent reading performance.

A more formal version of the repeated reading strategy, involving teacher or tutor and child reading in unison, is termed the impress method, neurological impress method (NIM) or 'read along approach'. Detailed descriptions of NIM can be found in Kemp (1987) and Westwood (1997).

## Listening to children read: the 'pause, prompt, praise' technique

A balanced and comprehensive approach to reading must allow opportunities for teachers and tutors to listen to individual children read aloud. Listening to oral reading allows the teacher to assess the child's reading strategies and to monitor such aspects as fluency and expression.

A technique known as 'pause, prompt, praise' (PPP) was developed by Professor Glynn and his associates at the University of Auckland for use when listening to a child read. The technique has been applied very successfully by teachers in many remedial intervention programmes, and can also be taught to parents, aides, peer-tutors and volunteer helpers in school to use with the children they are assisting (Wheldall 1995).

PPP involves the following simple steps.

1   When the child encounters an unfamiliar word, instead of stepping in immediately and giving the word, the teacher waits a few seconds for the child to work it out.

2   If the child is not successful, the teacher prompts the child by suggesting he or she guesses the word from the meaning of the sentence or from the initial letter of the word, or perhaps reads to the end of the sentence.

3   When the child succeeds in identifying the word he or she is reinforced by a word of praise.

4   If the child cannot identify the word after brief prompting, the teacher quickly supplies the word (children should not spend too much time attempting to identify any word as this disrupts fluency and comprehension).

5   The child is also praised for self-correction while reading.

In Wheldall's (1995) study poor readers made good progress when trained tutors used the PPP technique. When PPP was combined with specific instruction in phonics and decoding, average increases in reading age of nearly fourteen months after seven weeks of daily tutoring were reported.

## Silent sustained reading

Children differ greatly in the amount of reading they do at school with the most capable readers significantly outstripping those with learning difficulties. This is a serious problem, given that children with learning difficulties need to engage in more reading in order to experience the necessary practice that will lead to improvement. Schools do acknowledge the importance of regular reading practice and one strategy used to ensure that all children do have an opportunity to practise is silent sustained reading (SSR). SSR has also become a fairly typical approach to implement regularly for twenty minutes in classrooms where 'literacy hour' is part of the daily routine.

Fenwick (1988) was reasonably optimistic about the value of SSR, suggesting that when it was managed effectively children did indeed read much more text each week, increased their ability to concentrate and stay on task, and, in many cases, developed a more positive attitude towards reading. However, evidence on the benefits of SSR are inconclusive (Dymock & Nicholson 1999) and it must not be assumed that simply providing additional time for children to engage in independent silent reading will necessarily increase achievement of all children. Block (1999) suggests that SSR has often proved to be ineffective in advancing study skills and critical comprehension because the children are simply expected to read silently, without any clear purpose and without additional instruction to help increase their range of reading strategies. If SSR is implemented badly it can result in children wasting time. Often they may select books to read that are too easy; such material does not challenge and extend their reading skills and can lead to boredom. Conversely, in order not to draw attention to themselves, children with learning difficulties may select texts that are much too difficult for their own reading level. High error rate then leads to frustration and avoidance. Biemiller (1994) warns that poor readers often spend substantial periods of SSR time covertly avoiding reading.

SSR is potentially valuable but teachers do need to monitor and check that all children are actually engaged in reading during the time available. This may necessitate a rather different role for the teacher from that of the conventional one of 'model' who also sits and reads silently during SSR. In particular, schools need to consider that five sessions of twenty minutes per week amounts to one hundred minutes during which poor readers could have been receiving intensive instruction and closely monitored practice.

# 6 Teaching the basics: phonemic awareness, phonic skills and sight vocabulary

> Although understanding is the goal, children must develop effective and efficient
> strategies for reading unfamiliar words when they encounter them in texts
> … 10 per cent to 15 per cent of children routinely have difficulty in this area.
> (Allington 1998, p. 207)

Children with learning difficulties tend to have problems in three important interrelated areas: phonemic awareness, phonic decoding skills and word recognition. Poor decoding skills and limited sight vocabulary cause major difficulties with comprehension.

## Developing phonemic awareness

It has been stressed in previous chapters that all children need to have well-developed phonemic awareness skills if they are to make a smooth entry to the world of print. Phonemic awareness is essential for understanding the alphabetic principle and acquiring phonic skills. Many children with reading difficulties continue to have weaknesses in the phonological domain and usually need specific training to improve their skills. There has been a proliferation of commercially published training programmes for this purpose (for example, Adams *et al.* 1998; Blachman *et al.* 2000; Goldsworthy 2001; Munro 1998). This discussion is intended to provide only a brief overview of the skills typically included in phonological training.

Phonological skills can be developed in two ways: incidentally though oral language, beginning reading activities and invented spelling; and directly through games, activities and exercises with a focus on attending to speech sounds (Guppy & Hughes 1999). In most situations teachers will utilise both avenues for maximum impact.

The skills to be taught (although not necessarily in this sequence) include:

- rhyming – recognising words that rhyme and being able to generate a rhyming word to match a given word;
- alliteration – recognising words beginning with the same sound;
- syllable awareness – clapping out syllables and stretching out words to pronounce them with syllable breaks;

- identifying initial sound – isolating and saying the first sound in a spoken word;

- identifying onsets and rimes – breaking single-syllable words into initial sound and final sound;

- creating a word from a given onset – thinking of a word that starts with, for example, /bl/ (black);

- identifying final sounds – isolating and saying the final sound of a word;

- sound-blending – combining a sequence of phonemes into the word they represent;

- segmenting words into separate phonemes – stretching out a word so that each sound can be identified;

- exchanging phonemes to create new words – adding sounds to the beginning of rimes to create new words; deleting or adding final sounds to change words; substituting middle vowel sounds to create different words;

- mapping phonemes to letter symbols – acquiring basic phonic knowledge.

The published programmes referred to above all have a predetermined sequence in which the various skills are introduced and taught. However, children may differ in the order in which they acquire these phonological skills. It is generally agreed that sound-blending is achieved rather more easily than phoneme segmentation. Exchanging phonemes and mentally manipulating sounds in words is probably the most difficult skill to achieve.

Beyond the simplest levels, phonemic awareness training must be fully integrated with the teaching of letter–sound correspondences and related whenever possible to the child's attempts at inventing spelling. Castle (1999) suggests that training programmes to improve children's phonemic awareness should be given the following priority:

- identification of initial and final sounds in spoken words;

- segmenting words into sounds;

- blending sounds to make words.

She also suggests that phonemic awareness training and the explicit teaching of letter–sound knowledge to young children can significantly reduce the number of children experiencing reading failure.

## Teaching phonic knowledge and phonic skills

It is clear from the research evidence that helping children to develop better sensitivity to the phonological aspects of language is a necessary but insufficient condition to ensure success in early reading and spelling acquisition (for example, Ayres 1995; Torgesen, Wagner & Rashotte 1997). Phonological training appears to have maximum benefit when the auditory experience with speech sounds and syllables is combined with explicit instruction in letter–sound correspondences.

The training needs to progress to the point where the connections between speech sounds and letters are thoroughly understood and can be applied to decoding. For example, activities with onsets and rimes should link with the study of appropriate word families in order to facilitate acquisition of the orthographic pattern of the rime (for example, camp, damp, lamp, ramp, tramp, cramp, stamp).

Stahl (1998) observes that some educators regard 'phonics' as a dirty word, associating it with boring worksheets and mindless drill. Others regard phonics as the salvation of reading achievement. Stahl points out that phonics is neither of these things, but phonic skills are an essential component of skilled reading and need to be taught thoroughly to all children within a meaningful and integrated literacy curriculum. He suggests that exemplary phonics teaching:

- should occur early in a child's life;
- builds upon a child's awareness of print;
- relies on a good foundation of phonemic awareness;
- is explicit and direct;
- does not exist as a separate, unrelated set of experiences but as fully integrated in the reading programme;
- focuses on teaching ways of using grapho-phonic information in identifying words, not on learning complicated rules;
- includes explicit teaching of how to recognise and use letter-groups such as those used for onset and rime units and other orthographic patterns;
- develops other effective strategies for decoding words;
- aims to assist reading fluency and comprehension by ensuring the acquisition of automatic sight word recognition skills.

Finally, Stahl (1998, p. 215) states:

> Once a child begins to use orthographic patterns in recognizing words and recognizes words at an easy pace it is time to move away from phonics instruction and to spend even more time reading and writing text.

## Teaching phonics: where to begin

The basic principles of teaching phonics are summarised in Chapter 4. The following section needs to be read with those principles in mind.

Most teachers who devote time to explicit teaching of phonic skills usually begin with the teaching of single letter-to-sound correspondences – or as McGuinness (1998) prefers – *sound*-to-letter correspondences. Many children will have acquired some knowledge of letter names and sounds through incidental learning or home teaching during the emergent literacy period and teachers can reinforce and build on this knowledge. Some writers have suggested a particular sequence for introducing the letters (for example, Rubin 2000) but in practice the common letter–sound associations may be taught in any order.

When phonic knowledge is to be taught in a meaningful way from context, the order in which letters are studied is dictated by the nature of the reading material the children are using and the writing they are doing at that time. If phonic instruction is being given to children with reading difficulties it is, however, useful to heed the advice of Holdaway (1990) who recommends beginning with highly contrastive sounds such as /m/, /k/, /v/, /s/ and avoiding confusable sounds such as /m/ and /n/ or /p/ and /b/. It is also helpful to teach first the most consistent letter–sound associations (Heilman 1993). For example, the following letters each represent one sound, regardless of the letter coming before or after them in a word: j, k, m, n, p, b, h, r, v, w.

Identifying initial consonants can be made the focus of many general language activities in the classroom and this links easily with the phonemic awareness training that has included attention to the first sound in a word. For example, when children are consolidating their knowledge of single letter–sound links they can begin to make a picture dictionary or wall chart of items beginning with the particular consonant. Each consonant is given a separate page and the children paste or draw pictures of objects beginning with that letter. The 'T' page might have pictures of a table, tree, triangle, typewriter, television, tadpole. Children's names can be included on the appropriate page, either written by the teacher or by the child, and this can lead naturally to the introduction of pages for a, e, i, o and u: Alan, Arlene, April, Angus, Annabelle; Eric, Elaine, Eddy, Eve.

Resource materials such as *Letterland* (Wendon 1992) can be extremely valuable for teaching young children to remember the letter–sound correspondences. Alliteration used in the characters names in the *Letterland* stories help to create a sound–symbol link in the child's mind (Munching Mike; Ticking Tom; Golden Girl; Hairy Hatman).

Alongside or immediately after the teaching of single-letter knowledge it is natural to include the teaching of common digraphs (two-letter units representing one phoneme: for example, /ch/, /sh/, /th/, /wh/, /ph/) and blends (two or more letters forming a functional unit in a word, but in which separate phonemes are still identifiable: for example, /br/, /cl/, /tr/, /st/, /str/ /thr/).

Vowel sounds are far less consistent and predictable in their letter–sound correspondences. After first establishing by direct teaching the most common and regular vowel sound associations (/a/ as in apple; /e/ as in egg; /i/ as in ink; /o/ as in orange; /u/ as in up) variations are best learned later in combination with other letters when words containing these units are encountered (for example, /ar/ as in part; /aw/ as in saw and awful; /ie/ as in pie; /ee/ as in feel; /ea/ as in peach or, by way of contrast, as in great).

Learning the phonic units is of value – for example, in helping to guess a word from its initial letter or letters – but useful phonic *skill* requires that the reader be able to apply this phonic knowledge to real word-building and decoding. Abundant opportunity needs to be provided for learners to sound out and blend words (/b/ /a/ /t/ = bat; /tr/ /a/ /ck/ = track). This writer's experience as a remedial teacher suggests that sound-blending is a very important skill for children with learning difficulties to develop, and much time needs to be spent in raising the skill to an automatic level.

Weisberg and Savard (1993) have discovered that children's blending ability is greatly improved if they are encouraged to sequence the sounds in the word in rapid succession rather than pausing between each phoneme, as often happens with slow readers. The more slowly the sounds are produced the more difficult it is to hold the sequence in working memory and blend the word. Blending is also much more difficult if an intrusive vowel sound becomes attached to a consonant as the child sounds out the word (/buh/ /a/ /tuh/ sounds like 'beratter' rather than 'bat').

## Moving beyond the beginning level

For phonic knowledge and skills to become fully functional in terms of rapid word identification and spelling, children need to progress to the stage of dealing with letter groups (orthographic units). Experts in the field of reading development have advocated moving children to this stage of phonic skill as soon as possible (Cunningham 2000; Gaskins *et al.* 1998; Gunning 2001). Part of this learning may involve experience with compiling 'word families' (ill, pill, fill, bill, still, till, will, hill, chill, thrill). It may involve extensive practice in working with onset and rime units and reading and writing the phonograms associated with these (Strickland 1998; Cunningham *et al.* 2000). It may also involve the use of 'word sort' activities in which the children are given sets of words on cards and required to discover what makes some of the words the same (jump, stump, lump, hump, bump; camp, damp, lamp, cramp) (Bear *et al.* 2000). Word sorts can be made very simple; for example, requiring only the matching of initial or final blends (blue; black; blow; blind, blood); or they may be more complex in requiring the matching of words that sound the same but have different spelling patterns (meat, meet; pail, pale; no, know; road, rode, rowed).

Children's insights into word structure (and their confidence in word-building) can be significantly improved if they gain experience in working with commonly occurring letter strings to make words. Important phonograms that occur with reasonably high frequency, and are useful for such activities, include (adapted from Cunningham 2000; Stahl 1998):

| –an | –ap | –at | –ack | –ail | –ain |
|-----|-----|-----|------|------|------|
| –ake | –ale | –ame | –amp | –ank | –ash |
| –ate | –ay | –eat | –ell | –est | –ice |
| –ick | –ide | –ill | –in | –ine | –ing |
| –ink | –ip | –it | –ight | –oke | –ope |
| –or | –ot | –uck | –ug | –ump | –unk |

Valuable sources for teaching phonics and word study are:

*Phonics They Use: Words for Reading and Writing* (3rd edition) by P. Cunningham (2000);

*Teaching Phonics Today: A Primer for Educators* by D.S. Strickland (1998);

*Words their Way: Word Study for Phonics, Vocabulary and Spelling Instruction* by D. Bear, M. Invernizzi, S. Templeton and F. Johnston (2000);

*Patterns for Success in Reading and Spelling* by M.K. Henry and N.C. Redding (1999);

*Building Words* by T.G. Gunning (2001).

Also useful as a teaching resource is the set of material by M. Andrew (1998b) *The Reading/Writing Patterns of English*.

Commercially produced programmes such as THRASS – *Teaching Handwriting, Reading and Spelling Skill* (Davies & Ritchie 1996) are designed to ensure that children acquire a full understanding of the way in which the forty-four phonemes in the English language are represented by specific letters and letter groups. Comprehensive approaches such as THRASS, using direct teaching, are highly appropriate for children with learning difficulties who otherwise remain confused about the fact that the some sound units in English can be represented by different orthographic units (for example, /-ight/ and /-ite/) and how the same orthographic pattern can represent different sounds (for example, /ow/ as in flower or /ow/ as in snow).

It is necessary, of course, for children to learn at an early stage that not all words in English can be easily decoded using phonics, even when larger groups of letters are used. These 'irregular' words have to be memorised, added to sight vocabulary and recalled when necessary by a visual strategy. Some of these words are high-frequency words; for example, was, sure, said, any, ask. The teaching of such words is covered in the next section.

## Building sight vocabulary

The ability to recognise many words without effort increases a child's fluency, comprehension and confidence. Many words are added to children's sight vocabularies as a direct result of engaging in regular reading practice. The more frequently a child encounters a word in print the more likely it is that the word will be retained in long-term memory. Advocates for the purest form of whole language approach would argue that *all* words should be learned in this way and never introduced, studied or practised in isolation. Children who do not engage in as much sustained reading practice as others may, however, need to have sight words taught to them more systematically and directly (Fields & Spangler 2000).

One approach to the teaching of sight vocabulary is the use of flashcards. Each word to be remembered by the child is written clearly on a separate card. Games and activities can be devised to ensure that the child encounters sufficient practice and repetition of the words to achieve automaticity in their identification. To assist with storage of sight words children should also have a great deal of experience in writing the words while saying them aloud. The number of sight words practised each day by a child with learning problems must be carefully controlled by the teacher to ensure that the child's optimum learning rate is not exceeded (Talbot 1997). Attempting too many words is counterproductive – a fact not always appreciated by well-meaning parents when working with the child at home.

Sight words already practised on flashcards can be used for lotto games played by a small group of children. Each child has a card containing a different random selection of six words from a list of ten or fifteen words being studied at the time. The teacher (or group leader) picks up a flashcard and reads the word. If a child has the word on his or her card they cover it with a counter. The winner of the game is the child who first covers all six words *and* can read the words correctly back to the teacher. After each game the children exchange cards.

Nicholson and Tan (1999) report that increasing children's speed of reading words on flashcards can significantly improve their overall reading rate and comprehension of text. They also suggest that as poor readers get faster at reading words they become more motivated to engage in reading. This, in turn, gives them the practice they need in order to encounter even more words.

It is important to understand that there are two distinct stages in successfully learning to store and retrieve a word from long-term memory. The first stage is successful when a child can discriminate visually among the different words presented in a group or list and can point correctly to the target word when the teacher pronounces it. For example, 'Point to the word *breakfast*'. This stage uses 'recognition' and involves the relatively easy matching of an auditory stimulus to the visual symbol. The second and much more demanding stage requires not recognition of the word when pronounced by someone else but 'retrieval' of the word and its pronunciation from one's own memory. For example, when shown the word *breakfast* on a flashcard, the child must be able to recall unaided the pronunciation of that word. This process involves going from a visual stimulus to evoke a verbal output. Gaskins *et al.* (1998) suggest that to do this easily children need to be able to store not only the visual features (orthographic patterns) of the sight word but also the pronunciation of the word. They strongly believe that sight words are learned not simply from visual memorisation of the whole-word pattern, but rather through knowledge of letter pattern-to-sound

correspondences that help with pronunciation (for example, recognising /br/ and /ake/ in brake). Reading the nonsense words *farlam* and *stame* illustrates this tendency to identify unknown words from known, pronounceable letter groups.

Teachers often remark that children cannot remember sight words that have been taught already. This may well be due to the fact that too little time was spent in practice at the easy 'recognition' level before the child was expected to operate at the retrieval level. Effective teaching of sight vocabulary requires careful attention to both levels.

Poor recall may also be due, perhaps, to failing to attend closely to the most helpful cues within the word; namely, the letters and letter groups. Learning sight words is made easier if the teacher ensures that the child is aware of the salient orthographic features that help to indicate possible pronunciation of parts of each word. Gaskins *et al.* (1998) have developed a valuable teaching system in which children are taught to read a set of key words that are of high frequency and have common spelling patterns. The children are also taught that when they come to an unfamiliar word they should apply the strategy of using one of the words they know to help unlock the new word. This approach helps to establish children's attention to spelling patterns and also teaches them how to read unfamiliar words by analogy (Gunning 2001; Moustafa 2000). This type of training is of particular importance and value to children with reading difficulties who appear not to discover these principles for themselves.

So important is basic sight vocabulary to early reading progress that several authorities have produced lists of words, arranged in order of frequency, beginning with the most commonly used words (for example, Fry 1977; Gunning 2001; Kucera & Francis 1967; Talbot 1997). The lists can be used as a source for constructing games and activities and they can also be used as individual checklists to assess a child's basic word recognition skills (Mariotti & Homan 1997). A typical basic sight vocabulary list is provided in Appendix 1. A set of material by Mary

Andrew (1998a) *300 basic sightword cards* is available from the Australian Council for Educational Research (ACER).

Additional suggestions for games and activities to develop sight vocabulary in children with learning difficulties are presented by Polloway and Patton (1997). Brief periods of practice in sight word recognition can be an appropriate focus in peer-tutoring or homework activities.

While flashcard activities and word study do not, in themselves, comprise meaningful reading, if used as a small part of an early reading program they do help to address the specific learning needs of some children. Nicholson and Tan (1999, p. 168) conclude:

> Flashcards and repeated reading activities may be a useful addition to regular reading instruction. They are an extra and should not be a major part of the reading instruction given.

Word identification, whether it be by sight recognition or by the application of phonic skills, improves only as a result of engaging in a great deal of meaningful reading of continuous text (Cunningham 2000). There is no substitute for sustained practice at a high level of success and none of the activities described in this chapter will be of value unless the child can put the strategies to work independently while reading for meaning.

# 7 Assessment

> We watch how they go about reading and writing, and where they need help. You start with their strengths and then you move on to what they need to learn next. (comment from teacher, quoted by Burns, Griffin & Snow, 1999, p.141)

When a child is having difficulties learning to read it is essential to find out as much as possible about the child's abilities and difficulties in order to provide well-targeted assistance. Working from valid diagnostic information it is possible to tailor the teaching methods and the curriculum in order to increase the possibilities for more successful learning (Afflerbach 1998). The specific assessment procedures described in this chapter have a proven track record for helping in the identification of a child's strengths and weaknesses, and thus in aiding the planning of effective instruction.

## Changing emphasis in assessment procedures

The targeted skills and the follow-up teaching procedures suggested in this chapter may appear rather traditional or 'old-fashioned'. Assessments that attempt to look at separate aspects of reading ability, such as basic sight vocabulary, phonic knowledge, sound-blending ability, decoding and comprehension have been criticised by many reading educators. They regard such testing of specific skills in isolation as artificial and undesirable and argue most strongly against the use of standardised, norm-referenced tests in the assessment of reading ability (Cooper 2000; May 2001; Neill 2000; Tierney 2000). Instead, they advocate that reading should be evaluated more holistically, using mainly observations of a reader engaged in authentic interactions with print. The popularity of 'authentic assessment' is clear from the number of texts written on this particular theme (for example, Burke 1999; Montgomery 2001; Tombari & Borich 1999).

This writer believes, however, that assessing component skills of reading in children with learning difficulties can yield a great deal of very valuable and accurate information about their specific strengths and weaknesses. Trying to obtain such information entirely from authentic reading and writing activities is a less efficient way of tapping a child's full range of skills and strategies. For example, if one wishes to determine a child's grasp of the first 100 sight words and identify which of these high-frequency words a child does not recognise, an appropriate word list is going to yield more complete and accurate information than trying to judge sight vocabulary subjectively from oral reading of a passage of connected text. A similar argument applies to other key components of reading, such as phonic knowledge and decoding skills.

This writer also supports the occasional judicious use of standardised testing to assess a child's progress in comparison with his or her age group, for purposes of monitoring standards in literacy within and across schools, and to provide data that may help a school prove a case for additional support and resources.

## The purposes for testing

Hempenstall (1998) has suggested that the purposes for assessment in reading include:

- diagnosing particular areas of strength or weakness;
- using the information for decisions about instruction;
- measuring a child's progress over a period of time;
- comparing one child's progress to that of his or her peers;
- screening children for special assistance.

Each of these purposes will be explored briefly, with most attention devoted to the diagnostic and programme-planning aspects.

## Basic principles of diagnostic assessment

A useful starting point for the assessment of children with learning difficulties is to obtain data to answer the following four questions. These basic questions can be applied to functional assessment in any school subject (Westwood 1997). It should be noted that the questions focus on learning and performance within the curriculum and not on so-called 'cognitive or perceptual deficits' within the child:

1. For this subject area (reading) what can the child already do unaided; that is, what knowledge, skills and strategies does he or she possess?

2. What can the child do if given a little guidance or prompting?

3. Are there any important gaps in the child's prior learning?

4. What does the child need to be taught next in order to make progress?

Answers to these questions will have direct implications for planning a support program. Information under these four categories enables a teacher to:

- build upon knowledge and skills the child has already acquired;
- prioritise what the child still needs to learn;
- select resources at the correct level of difficulty;

- fill any gaps that may have occurred in previous learning (due, for example, to frequent absences from school or change of school).

## Assessment procedures

The information required to answer the four diagnostic questions and serve the five purposes listed by Hempenstall (1998) can be obtained by:

- observation
- working individually with a child
- using diagnostic procedures
- applying formal and informal testing.

In practice, all four procedures may be used in combination to discover as much as possible about the instructional needs of a child with learning difficulties.

### Observation

Planned observation represents a very important and natural means of discovering a child's strengths and weaknesses in reading and writing (Airasian 2000; Harp & Brewer 2000). Observation utilises the actual classroom literacy tasks children are required to engage in during lesson time (Burke 1999).

Tindal and Marston (1990) have concluded that observations are often considered more useful than standardised testing because they can be made unobtrusively and they yield information that more formal testing instruments cannot obtain.

They also provide valuable supplementary information in such areas as the child's application of knowledge, use of particular reading strategies, self-correction, initiative and on-task behaviour. Linn and Gronlund (1995) comment that direct observation is the only means available for evaluating some qualitative aspects of learning and development. In particular, observation is important for assessing work habits, attitudes, confidence, interests and children's self-management – all of which contribute to effective literacy learning.

### Checklists and inventories

Observation in the classroom may be carried out informally or more formally by using a checklist to target the appraisal of specific behaviours and skills. To facilitate observation and recording of children's abilities, inventories or checklists may be designed by the teacher to contain a selection of items that cover the desired range of knowledge and skills (Afflerbach 1998; Mariotti & Homan 2001). For example, the information in the Reading Benchmark descriptors (see p. 90) could be converted into an observation checklist to aid the appraisal of individual children.

Informal reading inventories (IRI) are valuable for assessing a child's independent reading level. Published IRI exist, but teachers can easily construct their own from a wide variety of age-appropriate books. The first page of the IRI might be taken from a relatively easy book with simple sentence structure and an illustration. The next is taken from a slightly more challenging text, and so on. These graded samples should help the teacher to identify quite accurately the level of text the child can read independently in class and the level of text that would cause high error rate and frustration. Listening to the child read the samples in the IRI will also provide additional information on fluency, word identification skills and confidence. The child's ability to summarise what he or she has read and to answer questions on the passage will help to indicate level of comprehension. The assessment battery devised by Swearingen and Allen (2000) is particularly useful for these purposes.

The information obtained from observing a child reading should guide the teacher in planning any necessary intervention programme, particularly in terms of building on the child's current abilities and teaching to fill any gaps detected in previous learning. To assist with this process 'running records' can be of value.

## Running records

Listening to children read aloud and using some form of 'running record' to list their responses is one of the most useful observational procedures for identifying precisely where a child may need help. Various approaches to reading error analysis (miscue analysis) have been developed over the years. Some of the approaches are overly complex and quite unnecessary for most teaching and programming purposes (for example, Goodman & Burke 1972). Others are more user-friendly and of immediate practical value (for example, Clay 1993; Cooper 2000; Kemp 1987; McGee & Richgels 2000). The book by Kemp provides some particularly useful examples of the way in which the key features of a child's oral reading performance can be recorded by the teacher and how some aspects of performance can be quantified to allow accurate measurement of progress or change over time (for example, accuracy, reading rate, dependency rate, self-correction rate).

All teachers trained in Reading Recovery procedures (see Chapter 8) make frequent use of such 'running records' of children's reading in order to determine the skills and strategies a child has already acquired and what needs to be taught next. The purpose for taking regular records of a child's reading skills is to help give clear focus to the planning of instruction.

It should be noted that to be valid and reliable, running records must be based on an adequate and representative sample of a child's reading performance. For example, running records for reading should be based, if possible, on not less than 300 words of text (Kemp 1987), although this sample does not have to be obtained at a single sitting. Conclusions should not be made about a child's strengths and weaknesses on too little information.

## Dynamic assessment

Cooper (2000) stresses that assessment should be an interactive process, with the teacher using additional probes and prompts to discover what a child thinks, knows and can do. Working one-to-one with the child affords an opportunity for the assessor to use what has become known as 'dynamic assessment' (Simmons 2000). The term 'dynamic assessment' is used to describe a situation where a relevant task is set (for example, reading a paragraph and answering questions) and the child first attempts to read the material unaided. The assessor observes the performance and, if the child is having difficulties with word identification and fluency, decides quickly what strategies or knowledge the child needs to be taught in order to overcome the problem and read the text more efficiently. These strategies are then immediately taught and he or she continues to read the same or very similar text. The assessor observes the performance again and is able to note the extent to which the child has been able to benefit from instruction and advice in the short term (Pressley & McCormick 1995). If the first attempt at re-teaching has not been very effective the assessor may try again, using a different method or providing additional practice time. Unlike standardised testing where exact procedures must be followed, with dynamic assessment the process is adapted and modified in the light of the child's responses.

Dynamic assessment is an example of a procedure that works within a child's 'zone of proximal development' (Swearingen & Allen 2000; Vygotsky 1962). Skills and strategies within a child's zone of proximal development are those that the individual can almost carry out independently, and only needs minimal assistance. They represent the most achievable immediate targets for intervention. The 'help' from another person is often referred to as 'scaffolded instruction' (McInerney & McInerney 1998) and it may come from the teacher, the child's peers or from anyone supporting the child's learning, such as a parent or volunteer tutor. Learning activities that fall within a child's zone of proximal development have a high probability of success, whereas activities beyond the zone are usually too difficult and may result in failure and frustration (Westwood 2000).

## Diagnostic interviews

Diagnostic interviews combine many of the features of observation and dynamic assessment. The interview involves discussion between the child and the teacher, usually focusing upon the reading and writing the child has been doing in the classroom. The interview allows for assessment of affective factors (the child's attitude, feelings, beliefs), as well as cognitive and academic factors related to the application of relevant knowledge, skills and strategies. Reys *et al.* (1998, p. 55) describe an individual interview as a 'powerful way to learn about a child's thinking and to give him or her some special attention'.

Information from diagnostic interviews and dynamic assessment should reveal any motivational or attitudinal factors that may have to be overcome in children who have experienced frequent failure. These factors need to be addressed within the child's intervention program. Dynamic assessment during the individual interview also provides an indication of the child's potential ability to benefit from one-to-one instruction, and will reveal the appropriate difficulty level for any texts to be used. This information helps the teacher to plan the objectives and methods for future lessons.

## Diagnostic testing

Diagnostic tests are designed to enable teachers to explore a child's existing knowledge and skills. They also facilitate the accurate detection of any gaps or weaknesses in the child's prior learning. Examples include:

- diagnostic tests of phonic knowledge, where all the letters and common letter-clusters are represented in the test items;

- decoding tests containing word lists graded from simple to more complex based on orthographic regularity;

- phonemic awareness tests containing a range of simple listening tasks that allow the tester to appraise a child's abilities in phoneme identification, rhyming, blending and segmenting;

- word recognition tests containing the high-frequency words from basic sight vocabulary lists.

For diagnostic purposes, teacher-made tests are often just as effective as published tests. They can be linked closely to the curriculum the child is following and can reveal any knowledge, skills and strategies needing to be revised.

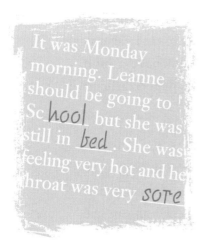

It is important to stress that in all cases of learning difficulty it is essential to go beyond the results obtained from standardised and diagnostic tests. The teacher also needs to appraise the suitability of the curriculum being taught to the child, the appropriateness of the resources and teaching method, the quality of the relationship between learner and teacher, and the physical and social environment in which the child is being taught. It is rarely sufficient simply to adjust the difficulty level of the reading material and increase the intensity of instruction. Often adjustments must also be made in the learning environment and to teacher–child interactions if progress is to be accelerated.

## Diagnosing prior instruction

It is vital that the teacher or psychologist doing an assessment should consider the adequacy and efficacy of the teaching methods and curriculum used previously with the child. It is now recognised that the learning problems of many children can be attributed in large part (if not entirely) to inappropriate or insufficient teaching (Burns, Griffin & Snow 1999; Pressley 1998; Pressley & McCormick 1995). Information on a previous teacher's methods is not always easily obtained, but whenever possible the assessor should find out whether the previous teacher favoured a child-centred, unstructured approach to learning or believed in direct and systematic teaching. In particular, did the teacher explicitly give instruction in word identification skills – including phonics and use of context? Often the results from the diagnostic assessment of such children will lead directly to the conclusion that what they need most is instruction that is clear, intensive, carefully sequenced and closely monitored for effects (Hallahan & Kauffman 2000; Hockenbury, Kauffman & Hallahan 2000).

## Specific examples of reading assessment

Listening to children read aloud from a suitable book at instructional level not only reveals a great deal about their confidence, fluency and strategic reading behaviours but is also a good starting point for a one-to-one assessment session. First the teacher may need to put the child at ease. This could be done by looking through some books together, discussing them and perhaps reading the first page of the material to the child before handing over the book for the child to read. While the child reads, the teacher should observe what he or she does when unable to recognise a word or when meaning is lost. Running records may help to summarise the quantitative and qualitative aspects of the child's reading. In particular, the teacher should be looking for evidence of:

- adequate sight vocabulary;
- decoding skills;
- use of context;
- self-correcting behaviour;
- comprehension at and beyond the literal level.

If the child shows signs of difficulty in any of the above areas, the teacher can follow up with some of the assessment procedures described below.

## Assessing sight vocabulary

Assessment of sight vocabulary has always been an important aspect in the evaluation of a beginning reader of any age. As indicated already, rapid word identification is the basis of swift, confident reading (Dymock & Nicholson 1999; Gunning 2001). Children must become automatic in reading and writing high-frequency words.

Basic sight vocabulary can be assessed quickly and efficiently using an appropriate word list with the child reading directly from the page or the words can be presented to the child on flashcards. The teacher needs to note any high-frequency words the child does not know, and these need to be taught thoroughly.

For example, Cunningham *et al.* (2000, p. 68) indicate that the following words – the, of, and, a, to, in, is, you, that and it – account for almost one-quarter of all the words children need to read and write.

Building sight vocabulary must be given very high priority in intervention programs. Flashcards still provide a very valid way of practising sight words. Use can also be made of games and computer software. It is, of course, essential to ensure that a child also practises reading and writing these words in a meaningful context. Practising sight vocabulary using the words only in isolation is of very limited value.

In the case of children with mild or moderate intellectual disability who may not be able to read aloud from a book, assessment of sight vocabulary is usually related to words in the child's environment.

Useful resources for sight vocabulary include those provided by:

- Gunning (2001, pp. 192–3) in *Building Words: A Resource Manual for Teaching Word Analysis and Spelling Strategies*. Gunning provides two lists – the first arranged by frequency of occurrence, the second in alphabetical order.

- Jones (1998) in *Curriculum-Based Assessment the Easy Way*. This text contains several useful word lists and word groups.

- May (2001) in *Unravelling the Seven Myths of Reading*. Frank May provides a copy of Fry's list of the 240 most frequently used words.

- Witt *et al.* (1998, p. 245) in *Assessment of At-Risk and Special Needs Children*.

These authors provide a list of the 50 most commonly occurring words derived from the Dolch list, the Brigance vocabulary list and the Durrell word frequency list.

Note: See also Appendix 1 for a list of high-frequency words and the words most commonly confused or misread by weak readers.

## Decoding skills

The research evidence overwhelmingly proves that phonic knowledge and decoding skills are essential for skilled reading (Adams 1990). Assessment of a child's knowledge of basic letter-to-sound relationships, including common letter clusters such as digraphs and blends, does not require published tests. The assessor can produce a checklist and a set of cards containing all twenty-six letters of the alphabet in capital and lower case. Other letter clusters commonly assessed include, for example, ch-, sh-, th-, wh-, ph-, cr-, tr-, br-, bl-, st-, sp-, str-. For children beyond the beginner level, it is also useful to assess recognition of the phonograms representing common rimes; for example, -eat, -ack, -oat, -ish, -end, *etc* (see Chapter 6). Common word-endings may also be included; for example, -ing, -ck, -ous, -tion. The cards can be presented in random order and a record kept of any letters not immediately recognised by the child (see Appendices 3 and 5).

If a child reveals a poor knowledge of phonic units, two steps must be taken. The first step is to check the child's phonological skills. As already explained, awareness of the sound units that make up spoken English is fundamental and prerequisite to the later acquisition of phonic decoding skills (Metsala & Ehri 1998; Walker 2000). It is usual to check a child's ability to:

- identify the sound at the beginning of a spoken word;

- identify rhyming words;

- split familiar one-syllable words into onset and rime (for example, /p/ – /ig/; /tr/ – /uck/);

- blend sounds to make words (/fr/ + /og/ = frog);

- segment words into their sound units (for example, stretch out the word 'van': /vvv/– /a/ – /nnn/).

For children needing additional help to develop phonological awareness a valuable resource is *Assessing and Teaching Phonological Knowledge* by Munro (1998).

Note: Two simple screening tests of sound-blending and segmentation are presented in Appendix 2. A list of common rime units will be found in Appendix 5.

If a child already has adequate phonological awareness, the second action that needs to be taken is the obvious one of explicitly teaching the letters and letter clusters that the child does not know and providing practice in sounding and building words. The provision of reading material with a high proportion of decodable words may be helpful at this stage, to facilitate transfer of phonic decoding skills to connected text.

A test containing pseudo-words is presented in Appendix 4. This test can be used to assess a child's ability to apply phonic knowledge and skills to decode unfamiliar words that are not part of sight vocabulary.

### Use of context

Assessment of a child's use of context can most easily be achieved through observation and listening to the child read aloud. Useful information can also be obtained from cloze exercises in which missing words must be predicted in a passage of connected text (see Chapter 5).

If a child is not making effective use of context (for example, not reading to the end of the sentence to try to predict an unknown word) the teacher should:

- demonstrate and discuss the value of using meaning, together with first letter clues, to help identify an unknown word in a sentence;

- utilise some appropriate cloze exercises to practise the prediction of a word from the sentence structure and meaning.

In both cases the teacher's modelling and use of 'thinking aloud' to demonstrate effective strategies will be powerful influences in helping the child adopt the strategies for independent use.

## Self-correction

When listening to a child read, the teacher should note the extent to which he or she realises when something is not making sense and, without prompting, pauses to self-correct any error. Self-correction is one feature of reading performance that can be quantified from running records (Kemp 1987). A measured increase in *self-correction rate* over a period of time is an indication that a child is benefiting from intervention and becoming more independent in reading.

The usual calculation for self-correction rate is:

(Number of self-corrected errors ÷ total number of errors) x 100 = ___ %

For example: a child makes sixteen errors but self-corrects four of them.

$$16 \div 4 \times 100 = 25\%$$

For children who do not self-correct (often those who have become overly dependent on the teacher or tutor for direction) it is important to:

- demonstrate and discuss how valuable it is to notice errors made when reading and to correct them;
- praise the child whenever he or she does self-correct while reading.

For children mature enough to understand the calculation of self-correction rate, this measurement carried out each week can be used as a motivating factor to encourage improvement. The child can set a personal goal to achieve. The same is true of calculating *error rate* (number of uncorrected errors ÷ total number of words read x 100) and *dependency rate* (number of times the teacher has to prompt, correct or in other ways assist the child ÷ number of uncorrected errors x 100).

## Comprehension

Comprehension should be assessed from a combination of silent reading and text that is read aloud. The questions may be asked orally, as in the diagnostic interview situation, or may be in written form for the child to read and answer in writing.

When assessing comprehension it is important to ask the child to summarise in his or her own words the main gist of what has just been read. This can be followed up with specific questions to cover factual information at the literal level, as well as questions requiring the child to interpret, infer, predict and respond critically to the material.

The standardised test *Neale Analysis of Reading Ability* (described on p. 89) is an appropriate test to use with individual children aged from 6 to 13 years.

It enables the teacher to assess comprehension, accuracy and reading rate. Teachers can, however, use any age-appropriate reading material as the basis for informal assessment of comprehension.

Salvia and Ysseldyke (1998) refer to three problems children may have in comprehension.

- They may approach reading as nothing more than a word-pronunciation task and so do not actively engage with the text to make meaning. This is particularly evident when a reader lacks automaticity in word recognition and is therefore very slow in processing the text.

- They have no effective strategies to help them process the information or to make meaning. They do not scan the text before reading to get an idea of what the material will be presenting and they do not think ahead. They do not formulate questions in their minds before or during reading and they do not reflect upon what they have read.

- They do not monitor their own level of understanding.

Depending on the child's age, there is a need in such cases to engage the child either in more shared book experience or in guided reading (see Chapter 5). The main teaching techniques involve discussing what is read, asking and answering questions, predicting, reflecting, criticising and summarising. Guided reading might also be thought of as 'teaching reading as a thinking process'. As indicated earlier, to improve comprehension it is essential to teach children comprehension strategies (that is, *how* to approach text in order to obtain the main ideas and the supporting detail, *how* to think critically about the information and *how* to generate questions and make predictions). Chapters 2 and 5 in this book provide additional guidance on improving comprehension. Valuable teaching suggestions for comprehension strategy training are also presented in the chapter by Wright in the book *Learning Disabilities: Advocacy and Action* (Westwood & Scott 1999).

## Standardised testing

Two of the purposes for assessment mentioned by Hempenstall (1998) – comparing one child's progress to that of his or her peers and measuring an individual's progress over a period of time – are usually achieved by the use of standardised, norm-referenced reading tests. These are published tests with set procedures to be followed in their administration and scoring. Criteria are provided for interpreting a child's results against tables of norms showing the average scores for children at particular age levels.

Standardised testing in reading became very unpopular in mainstream Australian education during the late 1970s and remained so throughout the 1980s and 1990s. This was due in part to the swing towards humanistic and developmental philosophies in teaching, and also to the adoption of constructivist theories of learning as reflected in whole language classrooms. It was felt that assessment should always be based on real classroom activities, not on contrived exercises and decontextualised tasks believed to be typical of published tests (Cooper 2000). There was also a suspicion that, for some children, standardised reading tests produced results that could be misleading. For example, children with disabilities, those from non-English-speaking backgrounds, or children from underprivileged families might, for a variety of reasons, produce results that did not reflect their true abilities. Finally, there was a fear that standardised testing in schools could cause teachers to 'dumb down' the curriculum by including only those activities that would contribute to increasing children's test scores (Calkins, Montgomery & Santman 1998).

By the mid-1990s there were signs that the potential value of standardised testing was again being recognised for such purposes as screening whole school populations for learning difficulties and checking the overall standards of literacy and numeracy across the country. Individual teachers use much less standardised testing now within their own classrooms than teachers did fifteen or twenty years ago. Most special educators and support teachers consider that there is still a place for this sort of testing in areas such as spelling, reading comprehension, computational skills and mathematical problem-solving. They fully understand, however, that the diagnostic value of information from these tests is fairly limited and such tests sample only a few aspects of a child's overall performance. They must be supplemented with data from more sensitive methods of assessment.

When standardised tests are given at the same time to whole classes or groups of children – as, for example, in the routine 'basic skills testing' used regularly in several Australian states – there is no opportunity to assess qualitative aspects of any individual child's reading strategies. The results provide mainly quantitative data on performance, although inspection of a child's test script can provide some general indicators of strengths and weaknesses and this information is often fed back to schools.

Norm-referenced assessments administered in this way do provide a useful indication of the overall standard of reading in each school and within each classroom. Data of this kind can be used sometimes to argue a case for additional human and material resources in schools where test results are well below state averages. Such measures of reading achievement are also invaluable for educational research purposes.

Standardised tests are not all designed for group administration. Some require that children be assessed individually, often by reading aloud to the teacher and answering questions about what has been read. A good example of such a test is the *Neale Analysis of Reading Ability* (Neale 1999) described below. When standardised tests are given in this way they yield not only quantitative data but also allow the teacher or tester to appraise qualitative aspects of a child's reading skills and strategies.

## The *Neale Analysis of Reading Ability*

This well-established and extremely useful set of reading assessment materials was first published in 1958 and is now in its third edition. The *Neale Analysis of Reading Ability* (NARA) is very popular with educational psychologists, guidance officers, school counsellors and teachers. The test provides norms based on the average performance of Australian children aged 6 to 13 years. NARA has proved to be a concise and very convenient tool for appraising a child's reading ability in terms of accuracy, fluency (rate) and comprehension. The individual testing of a child usually takes no more than twenty minutes. Neale (1999, p. 5) wrote:

> The Neale Analysis is designed to set up a dialogue between teacher and student to empathically explore ways of facilitating acquisition of literacy in its broadest sense.

Two parallel and equivalent forms of the main reading materials have been provided, to allow re-testing on similar but not identical texts. Each form uses six different narrative passages, graded in difficulty from simple to more complex in terms of vocabulary and sentence construction. The passages are read aloud by the child. The tester can prompt and cue the child to a limited extent, as specified in the instructions. The tester carefully records details of the child's responses on a record form as the passage is read (or later from an audio-taped version of the reading). Following the reading of each passage the child is asked questions by the tester. If a measure of reading rate is required, the tester must time the reading of each passage according to instructions given in the teacher's manual. Norms are provided separately for reading accuracy, reading rate and comprehension.

Inspection of the errors the child makes, as indicated on the record form, can sometimes be useful in determining what strategies he or she is using and what needs to be taught next in order to accelerate improvement. However, Neale (1999) and Hempenstall (1998) point out that detailed miscue analysis based on assumed semantic and syntactic aspects of a text is not always helpful in planning intervention. It is more useful to look at the child's errors in terms of what they reveal about word-attack strategies, phonic knowledge and self-correcting behaviours. If weaknesses are suspected in phonic knowledge and decoding it is advisable to follow up with more detailed assessment of these areas. The material in NARA also includes diagnostic sub-tests to be used with children who perform very poorly on the simple passages. These sub-tests examine knowledge and skills in identification of initial and final sounds, names and sounds of letters, auditory discrimination and sound-blending, spelling, word identification and silent reading followed by writing.

The teacher's manual contains detailed information and instruction on how to administer, score and interpret the tests. The technical section of the manual provides detailed evidence confirming the acceptable validity, reliability and standard error of measurement of the two forms of NARA.

## Benchmarks for reading

A somewhat different approach to assessing children's reading ability is reflected in the Australian 'Benchmarks for Literacy' promulgated in the late 1990s by the Commonwealth Department for Education, Training and Youth Affairs. Benchmarking is a strategy designed to help ensure that all children in the primary years reach a required standard of literacy. Those children with learning difficulties who are found to be performing below the benchmark for their age level are candidates for intensive intervention.

According to the official description:

> Benchmarks are a set of indicators or descriptors which represent nationally agreed minimum acceptable standards for literacy and numeracy at a particular year level. In this context 'minimum acceptable standard' means a critical level of literacy and numeracy without which a student will have difficulty making sufficient progress at school. (DETYA 2001, p. 1)

The reading benchmarks for the school years 3, 5 and 7 are presented below.

### Year 3

At the benchmark standard, children read and understand a range of texts that are suitable for this year level. These texts appear in, for example, picture books, illustrated chapter books, junior reference material and the electronic media.

Typically, texts that these children are able to read have predictable text and sentence structures and use straightforward, everyday language. Words that may be unfamiliar are explained in the writing or through the illustrations.

When children read and understand texts like these they can:

- identify the main purpose of the text (for example, say that the purpose of a set of short simple instructions is to help you do something);
- identify a sequence of events in stories;
- find directly stated information in the written text and/or illustrations;
- make links between ideas stated directly and close together in different parts of a text (for example, predict the end of a story, work out a character's feelings from an illustration, make links between a diagram and its label);
- work out the meaning of some unfamiliar phrases and words.

### Year 5

At the benchmark standard, children read and understand a range of texts that are suitable for this year level. These texts appear in, for example, chapter books, junior novels, junior reference material, magazines, newspapers and the electronic media.

Texts that these children are able to read may have:

- varied sentence beginnings (for example, After ploughing, the soil is raked and flattened.);
- a significant amount of new vocabulary explained by text and illustrations;
- some long groups of words (for example, the largest planet so far discovered; a cute, well-trained dog; the edible seed of a type of pod-bearing plant);
- some use of figurative language (for example, his legs were turning to rubber; the wire swung and bounced like a live thing).

When children read and understand texts like these, they can:

- identify the main purpose of a text (for example, choose a title for a text to highlight purpose);
- identify the main idea in a text;
- identify the order of ideas and information in factual texts;
- find directly stated information in the written text and/or illustrations;
- make links between ideas in a text (for example, link information from a heading, written text and diagram; work out a missing step in a set of instructions);
- work out the meaning of unfamiliar phrases and words (for example, work out the meaning of figurative language such as her face was as white as a sheet).

## Year 7

At the benchmark standard, children read effectively for a range of purposes using texts that are common in the learning areas. The texts they read appear in print and electronic forms and include those that describe, explain, instruct, argue and narrate, often in combination.

Texts that children at the benchmark standard are able to read may have:

- new vocabulary, including subject-specific words (for example, papyrus, mummification) and words that create images and atmosphere (for example, grabbed, exotic);
- complex sentences that contain a lot of information (for example, The rainforests are filled with colourful parrots and there are beautiful little mice with feathery long tails, which hop along the leafy forest floors.);
- clear links between ideas and information within and between sentences (for example, This weighing was an important *test*: a good heart would balance a feather, a bad heart, full of sin, would not. The spells for surviving this *test* were contained in the *Book of the Dead*.);

- figurative language (for example, Spaghetti ends dribbled from his mouth like wet mop ends).

At the benchmark standard, when children read and comprehend these texts, they can identify the main purpose and main idea of a text and make connections between ideas and information in a text. For example, they can:

- specify that the purpose of a text titled *The Causes of Acid Rain* may be both to explain and to argue;
- identify the sort of people who would be the most likely target for the information in an advertisement;
- identify the moral in a fable;
- make a timeline showing the main events in a novel;
- identify some evidence used by a writer to support his or her argument;
- identify the reasons for a character's behaviour in a story;
- interpret the meaning of an unknown word;
- interpret a simple simile (for example, Spaghetti ends dribbled from his mouth like wet mop ends.);
- label a step in a flowchart.

The benchmarks described above are not 'test items' but rather an indication in broad terms of the abilities to be appraised at particular age levels by any suitable formal or informal assessment procedures. The same applies to *English: A Curriculum Profile for Australian Schools* (Curriculum Corporation 1994). These are not related to age levels but refer to the specific types of performance a student of any age might display when he or she has reached a particular stage or level of literacy development.

The indicators for any specific learning outcome are usually more detailed in the *English Curriculum Profiles* than in the *National Literacy and Numeracy Benchmarks*. For example, at Level 2 in the *Profiles*, under the 'text reading' category, descriptions of performance might be expressed in the following terms (adapted from Curriculum Corporation 1994, pp. 36–7).

Constructs and retells meanings from:

- short written texts with familiar topics and vocabulary, predictable text structures and frequent illustrations;
- visual texts with predictable narrative structures.

Evident when children, for example:

- comment on own interpretations of stories, informational texts, rhymes, songs, student-made texts;

- retell ideas from an informational text for beginning readers; comment on things learned or questions raised by reading;

- relate the story of a picture book, providing some supporting detail from the text and offering an opinion about the story or aspects of it;

- follow simple written instructions (for example, for using the classroom computers, a short recipe).

Under 'Linguistic structures and features', the child:

- has a bank of known sight words recognised automatically in printed texts;

- recognises letters and letter combinations that represent sounds in words;

- points out and explains the purpose of some organisational features of text (headings, index);

- recognises relationships in written sentences signalled by conjunctions such as 'because', 'and', 'but'.

The above items are adapted examples only and the reader is referred to the document for full details.

## Useful resources for reading assessment

Mariotti, A. & Homan, S. (2001). *Linking Reading Assessment to Instruction*

This resource contains many practical examples and applications of the teaching and testing concepts described in this book, including, in particular, the use of diagnostic interviews, informal reading inventories, cloze test materials, assessment of word-analysis skills and comprehension. Suggestions are also given for matching instruction to assessment information, and making decisions about grouping of children.

Miller, W.H. (1995). *Alternative Assessment Techniques for Reading and Writing*

This resource provides a range of informal assessments for classroom use, including observation checklists, word identification and phonics tests, error analysis strategies, oral and silent reading comprehension surveys and methods for exploring children's attitudes. Most of the materials for assessment of individual children can be reproduced.

Simmons, J. (2000). *You Never Asked Me to Read: Useful Assessment of Reading and Writing Problems*

This resource is mainly about the purposes of assessing reading and how the results can be used to improve instruction and learning. Case studies provide examples of assessments and their interpretation.

Swearingen, R. & Allen, D. (2000). *Classroom Assessment of Reading Processes*

This very comprehensive assessment battery, known by the acronym CARP, is based on authentic assessment principles and enables teachers to assess a variety of reading skills and strategies, mainly through the medium of graded passages (narrative and expository). The assessment involves children in listening, reading and the retelling of key points from text. Word identification skills are appraised and used as the basis for placing a child at the appropriate level within the text materials. Miscue analysis can also be carried out if desired.

Warger, Eavy and Associates (1994). *Reading Assessment in Practice*
A videocassette package, containing video, handbook and readings. Useful for teacher in-service work.

For teachers wishing to consider authentic assessment strategies, the following books may be of interest, in addition to those already referred to in this chapter.

Leslie, L. (1997). *Authentic Literacy Assessment: An Ecological Approach*

Valencia, S., Hiebert, E.H. and Afflerbach, P. (eds) (1994). *Authentic Reading Assessment: Practices and Possibilities*

# 8 Intervention and support

It is important to intervene to overcome reading problems as soon as they are detected. (van Kraayenoord & Elkins 1998, p. 157)

For many years schools have attempted to provide remedial assistance for children who were failing in basic academic subjects such as reading and mathematics. The traditional model is the employment of an extra teacher, full- or part-time, who provides tuition for individuals or small groups of children – perhaps only once or twice a week – away from the mainstream classroom in a separate 'resource room'. During these withdrawal periods the children receive intensive tuition to help raise their standards in reading, writing and mathematics. Many schools continue to provide remedial support in this way.

## Withdrawal versus in-class support

The overall impact of the traditional withdrawal model of remedial teaching has not been very impressive and has received much criticism (Collins 1961; Jenkins & Heinen 1989; Moody *et al.* 2000; Sampson 1975; Sewell 1982). Undoubtedly, some individual children have been assisted through the withdrawal model, particularly if they were in the hands of a highly skilled teacher and if the sessions occurred frequently, two conditions that are rarely met. Indeed, remedial teaching is often left to part-time teachers or volunteers with no training or knowledge in the field and the total time devoted to such teaching sometimes amounts to no more than thirty minutes each week. It is not surprising that for many children the outcomes are disappointing. This failure might need to be seen, however, as resulting from a lack of appropriate and sufficient instruction for the children at risk, rather than evidence that working with children individually and in small groups is not effective (Sampson 1975).

Evidence exists to indicate that, under the traditional withdrawal or resource room model, children with reading difficulties often find themselves provided with what amounts to a markedly inferior curriculum (Chard & Kameenui 2000; May 2001; Moody *et al.* 2000; Walmsley & Allington 1995). Rather than receiving the highly structured, success-oriented, fast-paced, practice-laden approach they require (Lloyd 1988), these children tend to receive simply 'more of the same' delivered at a slower pace. The researchers cited above have reported that children experiencing the traditional withdrawal model of remedial teaching:

- often have a diet of worksheets or exercises rather than sustained reading practice and guided reading;
- have a fragmented learning experience;
- engage in much less purposeful reading and writing activity than they would encounter in the mainstream class;
- receive little or no instruction in using effective reading comprehension strategies because the focus is entirely on low-level skill development.

According to the review of literature by Chan and Dally (2000), withdrawal models have been accused of:

- disrupting the classroom programme;
- absolving mainstream teachers of responsibility for helping low-performing children;
- stigmatising the children who are withdrawn from the regular class;
- failing to co-ordinate the remedial teaching with the mainstream programme;
- failing to increase the intensity of instruction and participation;
- having no lasting effect on attainment (even though short-term gains are often measured);
- being much too expensive.

Given these criticisms of the withdrawal model, it is not surprising that there has been a shift towards alternative methods of providing assistance to children with learning difficulties. The contemporary enthusiasm for inclusive education, with almost all children receiving their teaching in regular classrooms, has given

added impetus to this change. In particular, there has been a move towards much more *in-class support*, a greater emphasis on 'whole school' responsibility for supporting learning and an increase in collaborative consultation among teachers and other personnel (Dean 1989; Tiegerman-Barber & Radziewicz 1998; Walther-Thomas, Bryant & Land 1996).

Some schools now proudly proclaim that they *never* remove children from the mainstream for remedial teaching – the regular class teacher provides everything, with occasional advice from a visiting consultant or support teacher. Whether or not such a claim should be praised is open to debate. While many educators regard these changes as admirable, the removal of all opportunities to provide individualised, *intensive* instruction to children with learning difficulties is problematic (Mather & Roberts 1994). There can be no doubt that children who are failing to learn to read do require high-quality direct teaching and they need such teaching every day in a distraction-free environment. Is it possible for the regular class teacher to provide this, given that he or she must at the same time teach and manage a class? The answer is probably in the negative. In a study of inclusive classrooms, Baker and Zigmond (1995) observed that some essential elements of effective teaching are often missing or infrequently applied when teachers try to cater for a very wide ability range. For example, adaptations to meet individual children's needs are rare and close monitoring of children's achievement often does not occur systematically. Insistence on in-class support as the only approach to learning difficulties flies in the face of evidence that intensive one-to-one teaching produces the optimum gains for children with reading problems (for example, Pikulski 1994; Pinnell 1997).

Chan and Dally (2000) reached the conclusion that effective intervention for children with reading difficulties requires:

- highly trained professionals, capable of diagnosing difficulties and planning appropriate instruction;

- a programme in which children are taught the specific skills they need in order to cope with mainstream work;

- an effective teaching approach that accelerates children's acquisition of skills and strategies;

- the main goal of leading children towards independence in learning.

It is extremely unlikely that these requirements can be met through in-class support alone. There is still an essential place for remedial tuition in a withdrawal setting. Before adopting any doctrinaire policy that prohibits withdrawal of children from class, it is important to note that a study by Marston (1996) revealed that when withdrawal approach was *combined* with in-class intervention, teachers expressed satisfaction with the system and children made significantly better progress in reading. A support system that combines in-class support with some degree of individual or small group tuition, and also enlists parental support at home, seems to be the model recommended (very sensibly) in the policy document *Literacy for All: The Challenge for Australian Schools* (DETYA 1998).

## The principles of effective intervention

For more than a decade, the efficacy of literacy intervention programmes has been the focus of much educational research. Studies have yielded clear evidence of the main factors contributing to the best outcomes. For example, a study focusing on the middle school years and reported by ACER (2000) indicates that successful intervention programmes share many of the following qualities:

- school literacy coordinators with significant experience and knowledge of literacy providing education leadership, professional support and coordination;

- organisational structuring and timetabling that allow for flexible and varied groupings of children;

- teaching, in explicit ways, the curriculum literacies of each learning area;
- identifying and matching support to children's specific literacy learning needs;
- providing opportunities for children to practise reading a range of texts silently and aloud, and to write short and sustained texts;
- recognising the importance of fostering confidence and self-esteem;
- assisting children to develop more effective organisational skills;
- linking the support provided in out-of-class settings with the work of the regular classroom;
- acknowledging and celebrating children's progress;
- providing intensive support for children for a short period, or sustained support over a longer period;
- selecting reading materials and purposeful writing activities that engage children's interests;
- establishing effective links between home and school.

The results of the study confirm much that has been discovered about effective early intervention for young children in the first years of schooling. A review of these findings (Westwood 1998) reveals that the best outcomes occur when:

- time is spent practising important skills and strategies at high levels of success;
- instruction in skills and strategies is clear and direct;
- any negative behaviours being exhibited are reduced or eliminated (for example, task avoidance, hyperactivity, distractibility);
- a great deal of encouragement and corrective feedback is given;
- texts and resources are selected at an appropriate level of difficulty;
- in reading and spelling instruction, due attention is given to teaching both phonological awareness and phonic decoding skills;
- writing is included as an integral part of the literacy programme;
- use is made of other adults and peers to facilitate additional practice;
- close liaison is established with the parents or caregivers to ensure support and continuity of teaching approach.

In terms of the type of instruction provided, intervention research (Lloyd 1988) indicates that the most effective approaches for children with special educational needs tend to be:

- structured – characterised by a great deal of teacher direction in the early stages;
- goal-oriented – children are clear about what they are to learn;
- practice-oriented – new information and skills are repeated and applied many times;

- strategic – children are taught *how* to attempt the curricular tasks set for them;
- independence oriented – although *highly* teacher-directed in the early stages, learners are expected to acquire knowledge and skills that will enable them later to work and learn more independently.

To this list Phillips *et al.* (1996) and Torgesen (1998) would add:

- a brisk pace of instruction;
- variety in format of lesson presentation;
- maximum active participation by children;
- strategies used to motivate children and keep them on task;
- completion of all work attempted;
- use of regular formative (ongoing) assessment of learning against the objectives set for individual children.

To have maximum impact, a child's remedial programme should be offered *every day*, even if the session lasts for no more than ten minutes. Support programmes that are only offered once or twice a week usually achieve very little because intensity of teaching is too low and continuity is lost. Most of the research studies have indicated the great value of explicit teaching – but this must not be interpreted as meaning total domination by the teacher at all times. The notion of 'scaffolded guidance' is a better way of thinking about the role of the teacher (Marzano & Paynter 1994; Pressley 1998). The learner needs to be helped to make discoveries and take responsibility for his or her own learning. Too much teacher direction leaves the learner still dependent and lacking in initiative.

## An example of early intervention: Reading Recovery

Reading Recovery is an early intervention programme first developed in New Zealand by Marie Clay (1985; 1994). The programme is now used in many other countries, including North America, Britain and Australia. It targets children who are identified as having reading difficulties after one year in school. The aim is to work with these children as early as possible so that problems are overcome before negative attitudes and loss of motivation occur. The first and second year of school are said to offer a 'window of opportunity' to restore children's interest and confidence by accelerating their learning and preventing further failure. The children engage in a great deal of successful reading practice and are led to discover important concepts about print and how to unlock and use the code.

The children remain in the programme for approximately fifteen weeks or until they have reached the average reading attainment level of their class. They receive daily lessons in a one-to-one teaching situation with a specially trained Reading Recovery teacher. Each lesson lasts approximately thirty minutes. During this time the children engage in a range of activities designed to increase their word identification strategies and develop comprehension. While much of the teaching is explicit and direct, the children are also encouraged to think for themselves about print and language in order to gain control over their own learning (Pinnell 1997). The lessons are described as highly organised and intensive – but enjoyable. During the lesson optimum use is made of the available time and children are kept fully on task. Both reading and writing skills are covered in every lesson.

A typical Reading Recovery session includes the following activities:

- re-reading a familiar book;
- independent reading aloud of a book introduced the previous day (during this reading the teacher takes running records of the child's strengths and weaknesses in applying specific reading strategies);
- writing a message or brief story, with help from the teacher (who encourages invented spelling and 'listening to sounds within the words');
- working with letter-tiles or plastic letters to make words;
- sentence-building using word cards from the day's writing activity;
- reading a new book with the teacher.

Iversen and Tunmer (1993) report that children's progress in Reading Recovery can be enhanced even further if explicit teaching of phonological skills and decoding is included in each lesson.

The books used in Reading Recovery are selected very carefully to provide a gradual increase in difficulty from simple to more demanding, as well as abundant opportunities for the child to read a wide range of books at each level. The aim is to ensure a high success rate when the child reads the book unaided. Teachers trained in Reading Recovery procedures are taught how to assess the readability level of children's books. They are also trained to take regular running records of a child's oral reading performance as a diagnostic procedure to help determine what the child needs to be taught next and what strategies he or she has already learned.

Evidence has accumulated to indicate that Reading Recovery as an early intervention programme is very effective in raising young children's reading achievement and confidence (Iversen & Tunmer 1993; Pinnell 1997; Smith-Burke 2001; Trethowan, Harvey & Fraser 1996). It is claimed that the programme can be so effective that only 1 per cent of children need to be referred for further, long-term assistance with reading and writing. This level of efficacy has been challenged by some observers who believe that gains made in the programme are not necessarily maintained over time and skills taught in the recovery sessions do not generalise to the children's classroom reading activities (Wheldall, Centre

& Freeman 1993). These observations may reflect a failure to ensure that Reading Recovery strategies are continued within the classroom programme and that texts are still within the reader's capability.

A valid criticism of Reading Recovery is that it is very labour-intensive and therefore very expensive to operate. It represents the very opposite of using unskilled volunteers to provide learning assistance in schools.

## 'Success for All'

'Success for All', an early intervention programme designed in the United States by Robert Slavin and his associates, has also been adopted (albeit in a slightly modified form) in some parts of Australia. It uses intensive one-to-one teaching, using teachers or paraprofessionals, to help improve the literacy learning rate for at-risk and socially disadvantaged children (Woo & Morrow 2001).

Chan and Dally (2000, p. 226) describe the intervention as follows:

> The tutoring process in Success for All is similar to the Reading Recovery program in that its first emphasis is on reading meaningful texts. Initial reading experiences are followed by phonics instruction which provides systematic strategies for cracking the reading code. Emphasis is also given to strategies to assist and monitor comprehension, such as teaching students to stop at the end of a page and ask, 'Did I understand what I just read?'

Success for All lessons operate daily for twenty minutes. The teacher concerned also participates in the classroom reading programme and operates a reading lesson to ensure continuity, transfer and relevance of what is taught in the individual lessons. One unique feature of the pure form of Success for All is that the whole school usually has to regroup for reading, with children going to different classrooms for instruction based on their own ability level (McEwan 1998). This necessitates block-timetabling, an organisational demand that some schools are reluctant to meet.

As with Reading Recovery, research evidence in general has been strongly in favour of Success for All as an intervention model (Slavin & Madden 2001; Woo & Morrow 2001), although again some observers question its longer term benefits. McEwan (1998 p. 68) advises school principals that although Slavin's model is 'better than anything else available at the moment', the programme still is not entirely successful in developing the word identification skills of the weakest children. This problem is not unique to Success for All. It is widely known that a small, but hardcore group of struggling readers seem not to benefit as much as other children from intensive intervention (Chard & Kameenui 2000; Clay 1997; Torgesen 2000). Whether these few children have the 'double deficit' of weak phonological skills, together with poor storage and retrieval of verbal information from memory referred to in Chapter 2, is not yet clear. Further research is needed to discover the most effective additional teaching strategies required by this sub-group of failing readers.

The two intervention programmes described above help to illustrate the productive ways in which a knowledge of the reading process is combined effectively with teaching and time-management strategies known to be of most benefit to children with learning difficulties. For additional information, see Slavin and Madden (2001) or Morrow and Woo (2001).

## Peer-tutoring and paired reading

The most readily available human resource in the classroom is, of course, the children. Children can assist other children in all areas of learning and can help one another overcome some of their difficulties. Peer-tutoring, or peer assistance, has proved to be a very viable model of support (Cole & Chan 1990; Fuchs, Fuchs & Burish 2000).

In the literacy domain, peer tutoring often takes the form of 'paired reading'. Paired reading was originally intended as a structured system for use by parents tutoring their own children at home. It involves the provision of assistance in the form of a partner for a less able reader. More recently, paired reading has been expanded to include not only the use of a parent but also another student, a volunteer helper or a classroom aide (Hayden 1998; Rasinski & Padak 2000) and it has been developed as a class-wide model with all children involved (Maheady, Sacca & Harper 1987). The same model has proved to be very effective for 'paired writing' (Topping *et al.* 2000).

The approach calls for helper and child to read one text together, with the more proficient reader modelling good reading rate and expression. A typical paired reading session takes the following format.

- The child selects a book he or she would like to read with the partner.
- The two partners then simultaneously read aloud the first page or pages of text, with the more able reader slightly adjusting his or her reading rate to match the child's pace but adhering as far as possible to natural speed and expression.
- It is often suggested that the less able reader should point to each word while reading.
- If the child makes any errors, the partner points to the word and repeats it correctly.
- When the child feels able to read a sentence or paragraph independently he or she is encouraged to do so and given positive feedback.
- If the child encounters a difficult word, the partner waits about four seconds for the child to work out the word. If it is incorrect or unknown, the partner supplies the word and the child repeats it aloud.
- At an appropriate time, the two partners read together again.
- Discussion and questioning about what is being read occurs at appropriate times during and after the reading.

Guppy and Hughes (1999) report that paired reading used for fifteen minutes a day for six weeks can improve some children's reading age by up to eighteen months. Benefits have even been noted from only five minutes per night at home with a parent on a regular basis (Rasinski & Padak 2000). Hayden (1998) suggests that the main reason for the effectiveness of paired reading is that it involves much more than the passive listening to a child read. It is interactive, with the helper's role clearly to assist the child improve in word identification, fluency and understanding. All teaching is firmly based on meaningful reading of text in a relaxed and supportive situation.

Teachers seeking additional information on peer-tutoring and paired reading could consult the book *Paired Reading, Spelling and Writing: A Handbook for Teachers and Parents* by Topping (1995). The small booklet published by the New Zealand Council for Educational Research, *Peer Power: Using Peer-Tutoring to Help Low-Progress Readers* by Limbrick, McNaughton and Cameron (1985), contains some very practical advice. See also *Buddy Reading* by Samway (1995). The chapter on peer-tutoring in the book *Methods and Strategies for Special Education* by Cole and Chan (1990) presents some very detailed and useful information.

## Parental involvement

It is widely acknowledged that whenever possible parents should be actively involved in helping their children improve in reading (Snow, Burns & Griffin 1998). This is particularly important in the case of children with learning difficulties who need to engage in frequent and regular reading practice. Being able to read at home and at school provides opportunities for such practice and for the continuity of teaching and learning from one context to the other. Some parents may wish to help their children and are eager to know how best to do this.

Most parents, whether they realise it or not, need specific advice on what to do so that a reading problem in school does not become exacerbated by too much or inappropriate teaching and pressure at home. Parents are not necessarily natural teachers, particularly of their own children (Gillet & Bernard 1989). Without some guidance they may, for example, be too critical and negative in their comments to the child while reading, rather than encouraging and supportive. They may emphasise one particular reading strategy (for example, phonic decoding) at the expense of teaching the child to use a range of different strategies. They may not ensure that the child self-monitors for comprehension and they may fail to praise when a child self-corrects. Some parents tend to concentrate too much on the child's overt performance when reading aloud, rather than considering comprehension and meaning (Hannon 1995). Parents may also provide too much direct help, rather than encouraging the child to take the initiative and become more independent. A very big problem occurs when parents spend *too much time* on a tuition session at home (Branston & Provis 1999).

This usually results in the child becoming very fatigued, stressed or bored, and eventually rebelling in an attempt to avoid such sessions in future. If help at home is perceived by the child as unpleasant, it will not achieve any useful outcomes and may instead add to a child's negative feelings towards books and reading.

Having identified the potential problems above, it is still necessary to indicate that the involvement of parents in reading programmes at home and in school does have some very real benefits and should be actively encouraged. If teachers realise that parents do not automatically do the right things at home, they are more likely to give the parents useful advice. The nature of some of this advice needed is implicit in the previous paragraph.

- Teaching sessions at home should not go on for too long. Branston and Provis (1999) suggest to parents that 'little and often' should be the rule and recommend no more than twenty minutes each day. For some children ten minutes will be appropriate.

- Reading should be conducted in a happy and relaxed atmosphere (Bloom 1987).

- Attention must be given to making complete sense of what is read.

- Parents should read to and with the child, as well as requiring the child to read aloud unaided.

- Children should be encouraged to self-correct and praised when they do so.

- Hints should be given to help children identify words, rather than immediately stepping in and telling the child the word (see Chapter 5, p. 65).

- Pausing during reading allows the child to activate strategies necessary to identify a difficult word. Only give the word to the child if, after one prompt, he or she still cannot read it.

Teachers need to accept that *showing* parents how to do something is much more powerful than merely explaining it. A parent will rarely say to the teacher, 'I don't know what you mean' so after a verbal explanation the teacher assumes, wrongly, that the parent has understood the advice. Teachers may need to demonstrate:

- pause, prompt, praise technique;
- how to cue a child to identify a word;
- how to focus on building sight vocabulary;
- how to ask questions at different levels of complexity;
- how to praise descriptively (for example, 'I really like the way you went back and looked at that word again. Self-correcting is good. Well done!').

### Selecting a book at an appropriate level of difficulty

Some parents have the idea that a child will only improve if given difficult books to read but this is the reverse of the actual situation. In the beginning it will be useful for the teacher to send the child home with the book that is being used in school. Often a re-reading of this text at a high level of success, together with a discussion of what has been read, will be the most useful form of assistance from a parent. If children select their own books, or if parents choose books, they need to be aware that *independent reading level* means that the child should be reading the words at 97 per cent success rate. *Instructional level* (with help available) the success rate should be at least 90 per cent to 95 per cent. Below 90 per cent success rate represents *frustration level* (see Chapter 5).

## Listening to a child read

Demonstrate to the parent how, when a child meets a difficult word, the word should not immediately be read to the child or the child asked to 'sound it out'. By pausing, and if necessary then prompting, the child is encouraged to control the reading. When the helper jumps in too quickly, he or she is controlling the event and doing nothing to encourage independence. It is also important for parents to regard a reading session as a 'shared' activity, with the parent also reading some pages or paragraphs and responding to the text with comments and questions (Walker & Morrow 1998). Some of the principles of 'shared book experience' and 'reciprocal teaching' (both described fully in Chapter 5) could usefully be passed on to parents. The book by Branston and Provis (1999) has an excellent chapter on the topic of how to listen to children read.

## Utilising reading games and activities

The exact purposes of word-building and spelling activities need to be made explicit. The aim of most games is to provide practice and repetition without boredom. To achieve this aim the child must make many responses during the game, all at a reasonably high rate of success. Time should not be lost in arguing about the rules of the game, or waiting a long time for the next turn. Parents may even need to be shown how to use flashcards in various ways to help the child build sight vocabulary through repetition.

## Appreciating parents' efforts

Some parents are anxious, frustrated, or impatient when their child has learning difficulties. They need encouragement and support from the teachers to indicate that they are doing the right things and their help is valued by the school (Bloom 1987).

Unfortunately, it must be recognised that some children with reading problems come from homes where literacy standards are not very high and where parents may have so many pressures and tensions in their lives that they cannot find the time or enthusiasm to assist their children. As schools move increasingly towards parent involvement it is important to remember the genuine difficulties some families have. No parent should ever be made to feel guilty or inadequate because he or she does not have the time to assist the child or to participate in school-based literacy support. It is still the responsibility of the school to teach all children to read.

## Use of volunteers and paraprofessionals

All of the advice regarding parent involvement applies equally to ensuring high-quality contributions from paraprofessionals (for example, classroom aides, learning support assistants). It also applies to volunteer helpers in a school's literacy programme. Unless paraprofessionals and others are well trained and used effectively, there is evidence that their services do not have much impact on the achievement of children (Allington & Baker 2000).

Learning support assistants and classroom aides have a vital role to play in one-to-one assistance with children and they must work collaboratively with the teacher to plan work and agree on goals and methods (Tilstone *et al.* 2000). The sessions they operate with children must have clear structure and purpose (Woo & Morrow 2001).

Two resources, highly recommended for volunteer helpers, tutors and parents, are *The Reading Tutor's Handbook* by Schumm and Schumm (1999) and *Tips for the Reading Team: Strategies for Tutors* by Walker and Morrow (1998). Guidance on the effective use of paraprofessionals can be found in *Help in the Classroom* by Balshaw (1999) and *Teaching the Literacy Hour in an Inclusive Classroom* by Berger and Gross (1999). Several contributors to the book *Tutoring Programs for Struggling Readers* (Morrow & Woo 2001) have discussed ways in which paraprofessionals, volunteers and parents can be used most effectively to assist with literacy improvement. The book also contains valuable advice on the setting up of support programmes in schools.

## Support and resource teachers

Many schools have access to a support teacher (or resource teacher) with expertise in teaching children with special needs. In the past these teachers were used mainly to work directly with children for a few lessons each week, either in a withdrawal room or by going into the regular classroom to provide assistance to the children. The disadvantage of this model is that it does nothing to help the regular class teachers become more skilled in diagnosing children's learning problems and in delivering modified instruction to meet their needs. Instead, the problem is handed over to the support teacher.

However, the preferred role for support and resource teachers is moving more towards helping teachers, rather than working directly with children. The support teacher may initially work with a child to assess his or her instructional needs and give advice to the class teacher on how best to help the child in the regular classroom. The support teacher may help the teacher to plan appropriate objectives for the child's programme, give advice on appropriate teaching methods and help select materials suitable for the child to use. The support teacher may also help the class teacher make contact with appropriate outside agencies or services to obtain additional resources or information. At regular intervals the support teacher will check on the child's progress and discuss with the teacher future directions for the programme. These meetings may be either informal or more formal if the child concerned has an official individual education plan (IEP) and the meeting is related to IEP planning and monitoring. In such cases, other professionals such as an educational psychologist, school counsellor, principal and social worker, and the parents may be involved.

This changing role of the support teacher is described as being part of a 'collaborative consultation model' (Dettmer, Dyck & Thurston 1999). Under this model, children's learning difficulties are seen as a whole school responsibility, with a number of different individuals co-operating to create a network of support. The support teacher's role may include helping the school to establish an efficient support system and providing some in-service staff training to help all teachers become more confident in managing children's difficulties. The support teacher may also co-teach with some teachers in order to help meet the needs of several children in the same classroom.

For additional information on support teaching refer to Chapter 14 in *Commonsense Methods for Children with Special Needs* by Westwood (1997).

## The role of computers and information technology

Information technology has been, perhaps, the biggest single influence over the past two decades in education reform. It has resulted in significant changes to modes of learning and teaching for almost all children. Technology has had particular impact on the education of children with various types of disability. This is indicated, for example, in the survey of literacy and numeracy in children with disabilities (van Kraayenoord *et al.* 2000).

Language arts, like all other curricular domains, has felt the influence of computers and computer-assisted learning. The availability of word processors, for example, has enhanced enormously the opportunity for all children to create, edit and publish texts as an integral part of their language experiences in and out of school (van Kraayenoord & Elkins 1998). Teachers, too, have been able to prepare and adapt print materials for children more easily than ever before. They are also able to locate and use a wider range of sources of up-to-date information for their literacy programmes.

Wepner and Ray (2000) cite studies to show that using appropriate educational technology via computer delivery mode can:

- motivate children and facilitate high levels of engagement;
- improve word-attack skills;
- increase sight vocabulary;
- develop reading comprehension and study skills;
- encourage writing;

- provide feedback on spelling;
- facilitate repetition, overlearning and practice.

In general, word processors are valuable because they integrate reading with writing and require the child to interact with the text being presented or created. Computers are infinitely patient, allow for self-pacing, present material in carefully sequenced steps and provide immediate feedback. Children are required to be active throughout the learning session and are usually found to have higher levels of motivation when compared with other lesson formats. In particular, computers seem to encourage children to take risks and explore many important aspects of language and literacy (Labbo & Ash 1998).

Computers are a means of providing additional help to children with learning difficulties. In addition to the above benefits, for remedial support purposes computer programs can provide effective drill and practice opportunities, are useful in gaining and holding children's attention, and alleviate demands on the teacher's time and attention in the classroom (Chan & Dally 2000).

Rubin (2000) advocates computer-assisted instruction for remedial reading and writing activities, with the teacher or tutor working together with a child on an appropriate software package or while creating text. As with all other forms of one-to-one teaching, the aim is to allow the learner to take more and more responsibility for his or her own learning and to encourage use of initiative.

It is beyond the scope of this book to deal in any detail with information technology and its role in assisting children with learning problems in reading. No attempt will be made to recommend specific software programs for literacy skills or to identify specific websites useful as resources – such information goes out of date very quickly. For helpful advice on using technology to support reading and writing, see Cooper (2000). For an excellent overview of the role and value of computer-based reading instruction, see Chan and Dally (2000). Ott (1997) describes the various ways in which computers can contribute to the learning of dyslexic children. Several sections of the report edited by van Kraayenoord *et al.* (2000) provide a useful state-of-the art summary of technology related to literacy for children with various disabilities in Australia.

Teachers are advised to consult the most recent software catalogues and to discuss their needs with the information technology adviser or similar expert in their education department. Support teachers and resource teachers need to keep abreast of the latest software and materials that may help within the context of remediation.

By combining human resources with the use of appropriate technological aids the necessary support for children with reading difficulties can be provided. Without such assistance, children who experience reading problems in early years of schooling may well have to suffer the negative consequences throughout their lives.

# Appendices

## Appendix 1

### Sight vocabulary

#### Ninety-nine commonly occurring words

These words represent some of the words children are likely to encounter frequently when reading any type of text. The list can be used for informal assessment to identify any words a child does not know. The list can also be used as a basis for flashcard work and other games.

| | | | | |
|---|---|---|---|---|
| he | she | it | is | if |
| in | of | or | all | and |
| as | at | be | big | but |
| go | can | come | can't | for |
| get | on | the | then | are |
| any | am | did | we | up |
| this | that | you | went | to |
| look | little | like | me | make |
| my | no | not | said | saw |
| so | see | tell | has | him |
| her | had | here | good | day |
| who | will | when | with | what |
| they | from | boy | girl | give |
| have | his | many | want | was |
| very | where | them | your | some |
| old | one | our | out | over |
| house | how | call | by | down |
| don't | there | time | two | why |
| because | people | friend | more | play |
| thing | again | about | after | |

## Words often confused by beginners or children with learning difficulties

| | | | | |
|---|---|---|---|---|
| were | where | when | went | want |
| with | which | here | there | their |
| they | them | then | who | how |
| ever | every | even | | |

Reading and Learning Difficulties: Approaches to teaching and assessment

# Appendix 2

## Phonemic awareness

These simple listening tests can be used to assess the general ability of a child to identify and manipulate sounds as required in decoding and spelling. The child does not look at the lists of words but responds to the teacher's oral presentation.

### Blending

'I am going to say some words very slowly so that you can hear each sound. Like this: /aaa/ /t/ = at. /h/ /i/ /t/ = hit. I want you to tell me what the word is. If I say /i/ /n/, what do you say? Yes, = in. OK, Let's try.' (Sound the phonemes at the rate of one per second. Discontinue after about five failures.)

| | | | |
|---|---|---|---|
| 1  i – f | 6  g – o – t | 11  sh – o – p | 16  s – p – i – ll |
| 2  a – t | 7  m – e – n | 12  st – e – p | 17  b – l – a – ck |
| 3  u – p | 8  b – u – t | 13  l – o – s – t | 18  f – l – a – sh |
| 4  o – n | 9  c – a – t | 14  j – u – m – p | 19  c – l – o – ck |
| 5  a – m | 10  d – i – g | 15  t – r – u – ck | 20  c – r – u – s – t |

### Segmentation

'When I say a word I want you to tell me each sound in that word. For example, if I say "ran" you say "/r/ – /a/ – /n/". If I say "shop" you say "/sh/ – /o/ – – /p/".'

| | | |
|---|---|---|
| 1  cat | 6  that | 11  face |
| 2  man | 7  step | 12  sing |
| 3  red | 8  help | 13  brush |
| 4  hot | 9  book | 14  string |
| 5  bus | 10  flag | 15  table |

### Initial sound

'I am going to say some words. I want you to tell me the sound that begins each word. Like this. Monkey: mmmmonkey. Monkey begins with /m/. Stop: sssstop. Stop begins with /s/.'

| | | |
|---|---|---|
| 1  house | 6  fish | 11  swing |
| 2  table | 7  little | 12  trees |
| 3  bag | 8  red | 13  chips |
| 4  cake | 9  dog | 14  blue |
| 5  water | 10  egg | 15  school |

## Onset and rime

'I am going to say a word. Then I am going to say the word in two parts like this. Ball: /b/ /all/. Train: /tr/ /ain/. Shop: /sh/ /op/. Your turn now.'

| | | | | | |
|---|---|---|---|---|---|
| 1 | man | 6 | dish | 11 | first |
| 2 | hit | 7 | sack | 12 | shelf |
| 3 | book | 8 | tell | 13 | cliff |
| 4 | cut | 9 | best | 14 | stand |
| 5 | lap | 10 | lunch | 15 | blink |

# Appendix 3

## Phonic units

These units can be used for assessment purposes to determine a child's basic phonic knowledge.

| | | | | |
|---|---|---|---|---|
| A | a | a | B | b |
| c | D | d | d | E |
| e | F | f | G | G |
| g | g | H | h | I |
| i | J | j | K | k |
| L | l | M | m | N |
| n | O | P | p | Q |
| q | q | R | r | S |
| T | t | t | U | u |
| V | v | W | X | Y |
| y | y | Z | z | 3 |

## Common initial consonant digraphs

| | | |
|---|---|---|
| sh | th | ch |
| wh | qu | ph |

## Common consonant blends

| | | |
|---|---|---|
| st | sp | sc |
| sk | sl | sw |
| sn | sm | br |
| bl | cr | dr |
| pr | tr | gr |
| fr | pl | cl |
| fl | gl | tw |

## Common three-letter blends

| | | |
|---|---|---|
| str | spl | thr |
| scr | shr | spr |
| squ | | |

Reading and Learning Difficulties: Approaches to teaching and assessment

## Sounding and blending pseudo-words

The following list may be used to assess a child's ability to use basic phonic knowledge to sound and build nonsense words. The use of nonsense words rather than real words eliminates the possibility that the child can recognise the word by sight. This informal assessment enables the teacher to appraise a child's decoding skills without the support of meaning and context.

Note: Some children will believe that they should try to say a 'real' word. In such cases, provide extra demonstrations to show that the word is not a real word and is not supposed to be a real word.

### Demonstration items

'In this puzzle we are going to read some words you have never seen before. They are not real words. Listen as I read the first three words. I will sound them out.'

| mep | /m/ | /e/ | /p/ | = mep |
|-----|-----|-----|-----|-------|
| sut | /s/ | /u/ | /t/ | = sut |
| bof | /b/ | /o/ | /f/ | = bof |

'Now you look at these words and sound them out.'

| lem | bup | raz | tog | hif |
|-----|-----|-----|-----|-----|
| dop | mig | sul | ked | vit |
| wep | jum | yun | neb | vos |

If the child performs well on the set of nonsense words above the following list can be used involving initial and final consonant blends and digraphs:

| spack | skump | stach | shull | treff |
|-------|-------|-------|-------|-------|
| glost | blift | crult | clitch | prelk |
| brunk | grusk | smoft | whalf | tweck |

## Appendix 5

## Common rime units

These units can be used for assessment purposes or for teaching. By adding a letter or letters to the front of these phonograms different words can be made. The phonograms can be used for word family activities and games.

| | | | | |
|---|---|---|---|---|
| –an | –ap | –at | –ad | –ag |
| –am | –ed | –eg | –en | –et |
| –ib | –id | –in | –it | –ip |
| –ob | –od | –og | –op | –ot |
| –ub | –ug | –um | –un | –up |
| –ut | –ack | –ail | –ain | –ake |
| –ale | –ame | –and | –amp | –ank |
| –ash | –ate | –ask | –ay | –eat |
| –eck | –ell | –est | –esh | –imp |
| –ice | –ick | –ide | –ill | –ine |
| –ing | –ink | –ight | –ock | –oke |
| –ope | –uck | –ump | –unk | –ung |

## Other common letter strings

| | | | | |
|---|---|---|---|---|
| –ight | –ough | –ought | –aught | –dge |
| –ance | –ence | –ange | –ose | –are |
| –tion | –ttle | –ddle | –tter | –bble |
| –cket | –ckle | –stle | –able | –ture |
| –ssion | –ible | –ious | –ent | –tial |
| –cial | –erve | –ieve | –tor | –tain |

# References

ACER (Australian Council for Educational Research) (2000). Improving literacy learning in the middle years of school. *Research Developments*, 5: 2–3.

Adams, M.J. (1990). *Beginning to Read: Thinking and Learning about Print*. Cambridge, MA: MIT Press.

Adams, M.J. (1998). The three-cueing system. In J. Osborne and F. Lehr (eds) *Literacy for All: Issues in Teaching and Learning* (pp. 73–99). New York: Guilford.

Adams, M.J., Foorman, B.R., Lundberg, I. and Beeler, T. (1998). *Phonemic Awareness in Young Children: A Classroom Curriculum*. Baltimore: Brookes.

Adams, M.J., Treiman, R. and Pressley, M. (1998) Reading, writing and literacy. In W. Damon (ed.) *Handbook of Child Psychology* (5th edn, vol. 4, pp. 275–355). New York: Wiley.

Afflerbach, P. (1998). Reading assessment and learning to read. In J. Osborne and F. Lehr (eds) *Literacy for All: Issues in Teaching and Learning* (pp. 239–63). New York: Guilford.

Airasian, P.W. (2000). *Assessment in the Classroom* (2nd edn). New York: McGraw-Hill.

Allington, R.L. (ed.) (1998). *Teaching Struggling Readers: Articles from* The Reading Teacher. Newark: DE: International Reading Association.

Allington, R.L. and Baker, K. (1999). Best practices in literacy instruction for children with special needs. In L.B. Gambrell, L.M. Morrow, S.B. Neuman and M. Pressley (eds) *Best Practices in Literacy Instruction* (pp. 292–310). New York: Guilford.

American Psychiatric Association (1994). *Diagnostic and Statistical Manual of Mental Disorders* (DSM-IV). Washington, DC: APA.

Andrew, M. (1998a). *300 Basic Sightword Cards*. Melbourne: Australian Council for Educational Research.

Andrew, M. (1998b). *The Reading/Writing Patterns of English*. Melbourne: Australian Council for Educational Research.

AREA (2000). 'Public education in the next generation': Submission to the Ministerial Working Party on Education. *Australian Journal of Learning Disabilities*, 5 (4): 4–7.

Ashman, A. and Elkins, J. (1998). *Educating Children with Special Needs* (3rd edn). Sydney: Prentice Hall.

Ayers, L. (1995). The efficacy of three training conditions on phonological awareness of kindergarten children and the longitudinal effect of each on later reading acquisition. *Reading Research Quarterly*, 30 (4): 604–6.

Baker, J.M. and Zigmond, N. (1995). The meaning and practice of inclusion for students with learning disabilities. *Journal of Special Education*, 29 (2): 163–80.

Balota, D. and Rayner, K. (1991). Word recognition processes in foveal and parafoveal vision. In D. Besner and G.W. Humphreys (eds) *Basic Processes in Reading: Visual Word Recognition* (pp. 198–232). Hillsdale, NJ: Erlbaum.

Balshaw, M. (1999). *Help in the Classroom* (2nd edn). London: Fulton.

Bannatyne, A. (1971). *Language, Reading and Learning Disabilities*. Springfield, IL: Thomas.

Barron, R.W. (1994). The sound-to-spelling connection: Orthographic activation in auditory word recognition and its implications for the acquisition of phonological awareness and literacy skills. In V.W. Berninger (ed.) *The Varieties of Orthographic Knowledge* (pp. 219–42). Dordrecht: Kluwer.

Bear, D., Invernizzi, M., Templeton, S. and Johnston, F. (2000). *Words their Way: Word Study for Phonics, Vocabulary, and Spelling Instruction* (2nd edn). Upper Saddle River, NJ: Merrill.

Berger, A. and Gross, J. (eds) (1999). *Teaching the Literacy Hour in an Inclusive Classroom*. London: Fulton.

Berger, A., Henderson, J. and Morris, D. (1999). *Implementing the Literacy Hour for Pupils with Learning Difficulties*. London: Fulton.

Berninger, V.W. (1995). Has the phonological recoding model of reading acquisition and reading disability led us astray? *Issues in Education*, 1 (1): 59–63.

Besner, D. and Humphreys, G. (eds) (1991). *Basic Processes in Reading: Visual Word Recognition*. Hillsdale, NJ: Erlbaum.

Biemiller, A. (1994). Some observations on beginning reading instruction. *Educational Psychologist*, 29 (4): 203–9.

Birsh, J.R. (1999). *Multisensory Teaching of Basic Language Skills*. Baltimore: Brookes.

Blachman, B.A., Ball, E.W., Black, R. and Tangel, D.M. (2000). *Road to the Code: A Phonological Program for Young Children*. Baltimore: Brookes.

Blair-Larsen, S.M. and Williams, K.A. (eds) (1999). *The Balanced Reading Program*. Newark, DE: International Reading Association.

Block, C.C. (1999). Comprehension: Crafting understanding. In L. Gambrell, L.M. Morrow, S.B. Neuman and M. Pressley (eds) *Best Practices in Literacy Instruction* (pp. 98–118). New York: Guilford.

Bloom, W. (1987). *Partnerships with Parents in Reading*. London: Hodder and Stoughton.

Boder, E. (1970). Developmental dyslexia: A new diagnostic approach based on the identification of three subtypes. *Journal of School Health*, 40: 289–90.

Branston, P. and Provis, M. (1999). *Children and Parents Enjoying Reading*. London: Fulton.

Browne, A. (1998). *A Practical Guide to Teaching Reading in the Early Years*. London: Chapman.

Burke, K. (1999). *How to Assess Authentic Learning* (3rd edn). Arlington Heights, IL: Skylight Press.

Burns, M., Griffin, P. and Snow, C. (1999). *Starting Out Right: A Guide to Promoting Children's Reading Success*. Washington, DC: National Academy Press.

Bus, A.G. and van Ijzendoorn, M.H. (1999). Phonological awareness and early reading: A meta-analysis of experimental training studies. *Journal of Educational Psychology*, 91 (3): 403–14.

Byrne, B. (1998). *The Foundation of Literacy*. Hove: Psychology Press.

Calkins, L., Montgomery, K. and Santman, D. (1998). *A Teacher's Guide to Standardized Reading Tests*. Portsmouth, NH: Heinemann.

Cambourne, B. (1988). *The Whole Story: Natural Learning and the Acquisition of Literacy*. Auckland: Scholastic.

Carver, R.P. (2000). *The Causes of High and Low Reading Achievement*. Mahwah, NJ: Erlbaum.

Castle, J.M. (1999). Learning and teaching phonological awareness. In G.B. Thompson and T. Nicholson (eds) *Learning to Read: Beyond Phonics and Whole Language* (pp. 55–73). New York: Teachers College Press.

Castles, A. and Coltheart, M. (1993). Varieties of developmental dyslexia. *Cognition*, 47: 149–80.

Chall, J. (1967) *Learning to Read: The Great Debate*. New York: McGraw-Hill.

Chall, J. (1995). Ahead to the Greeks. *Issues in Education*, 1 (1): 83–5.

Chan, L. and Dally, K. (2000). Review of literature. In W. Louden, L. Chan, J. Elkins, D. Greaves, H. House, M. Milton, S. Nichols, M. Rohl, J. Rivalland and C. van Kraayenoord (eds) *Mapping the Territory: Primary Students with Learning Difficulties in Literacy and Numeracy – Analysis* (vol. 2, pp. 161–331). Canberra: Department of Education, Training and Youth Affairs.

Chard, D.J. and Kameenui, E.J. (2000). Struggling first-grade readers: The frequency and progress of their reading. *Journal of Special Education*, 34 (1): 28–38.

Cheng, P.W. (1998). Primary school teachers' perceptions and understanding of learning difficulties. In D.W. Chan (ed.) *Helping Students with Learning Difficulties* (pp. 121–34). Hong Kong: Chinese University Press.

Church, R.P., Fessler, M.A. and Bender, M. (1998). Diagnosis and remediation of dyslexia. In B.K. Shapiro, P.J. Accardo and A.J. Capute (eds) *Specific Reading Disability: A View of the Spectrum* (pp. 171–96). Timonium, MD: York Press.

Clay, M.M. (1985). *The Early Detection of Reading Difficulties*. Auckland: Heinemann.

Clay, M.M. (1993). *An Observational Survey of Early Literacy Achievement*. Portsmouth, NH: Heinemann.

Clay, M.M. (1994). *A Guidebook for Reading Recovery Teachers*. Portsmouth, NH: Heinemann.

Clay, M.M. (1997). The development of literacy difficulties. In V. Edwards and D. Corson (eds) *Encyclopedia of Language and Education* (vol. 2, pp. 37–46). Dordrecht: Kluwer.

Cole, P. and Chan, L. (1990). *Methods and Strategies for Special Education*. New York: Prentice Hall.

Collins, J.E. (1961). *The Effects of Remedial Education*. Edinburgh: Oliver and Boyd.

Connelly, E.R. (1999). *A World Upside Down and Backwards: Reading and Learning Disorders*. Philadelphia: Chelsea House.

Cooper, J.D. (2000). *Literacy: Helping Children Construct Meaning* (4th edn.). Boston: Houghton Mifflin.

Critchley, M. (1981). Dyslexia: An overview. In G.T. Pavlidis and T.R. Miles (eds) *Dyslexia: Research and its Applications to Education* (pp. 1–11). Chichester: Wiley.

Cunningham, J.W. (1999). How we can achieve best practices in literacy instruction. In L. Gambrell, L.M. Morrow, S.B. Neuman and M. Pressley (eds) *Best Practices in Literacy Instruction* (pp. 34–45). New York: Guilford.

Cunningham, P. (2000). *Phonics they Use: Words for Reading and Writing* (3rd edn). New York: Longman.

Cunningham, P., Moore, S., Cunningham, J. and Moore, D. (2000). *Reading and Writing in Elementary Classrooms* (4th edn). New York: Longman.

Curriculum Corporation (1994). *English: A Curriculum Profile for Australian Schools*. Melbourne: Curriculum Corporation.

Dahl, K.L. and Freppon, P.A. (1995). A comparison of inner-city children's interpretations of reading and writing instruction in the early grades in skills-based and whole language classrooms. *Reading Research Quarterly*, 30: 50–74.

Davies, A. and Ritchie, D. (1996). *THRASS (Teaching Handwriting, Reading and Spelling Skills)*. London: Collins Educational.

Dean, J. (1989). *Special Needs in the Secondary School: A Whole School Approach*. London: Routledge.

Denckla, M.B. (1972). Clinical syndromes in learning disabilities: The case for 'splitting' vs. 'lumping'. *Journal of Learning Disabilities*, 5: 401–6.

Dettmer, P., Dyck, N. and Thurston, L. (1999). *Consultation, Collaboration and Teamwork for Students with Special Needs* (3rd edn). Boston: Allyn and Bacon.

DETYA (Department of Education, Training and Youth Affairs) (1998). *Literacy for All: The Challenge for Australian Schools*. Canberra: Commonwealth Government Printing Service.

DETYA (2001). *National Literacy and Numeracy Benchmarks*. Canberra: Commonwealth Government Printing Service.

Dombey, H. (1999). Towards a balanced approach to phonics teaching. *Reading*, 33 (2): 52–8.

Doris, J.L. (1998). Dyslexia: The evolution of a concept. In B.K. Shapiro, P.J. Accardo and A.J. Capute (eds) *Specific Reading Disability: A View of the Spectrum* (pp. 3–20). Timonium, MD: York Press.

Dunn-Rankin, P. (1985). Perceptual characteristics of words. In R. Groner, G.W. McConkie and C. Menz (eds) *Eye Movements and Human Information Processing* (pp. 111–35). Amsterdam: Elsevier.

Dymock, S. and Nicholson, T. (1999). *Reading Comprehension: What Is It?* Wellington: New Zealand Council for Educational Research.

Education Department of Western Australia (1984). *The Education of Children with Specific Reading Disabilities in Western Australia*. Perth: The Education Department.

Ehri, L.C. (1997). Sight word learning in normal readers and dyslexics. In B.A. Blachman (ed.) *Foundations of Reading Acquisition and Dyslexia* (pp. 163–98). Mahwah, NJ: Erlbaum.

Ehri, L.C. (1998). Grapheme-phoneme knowledge is essential for learning to read words in English. In J. Metsala and L.C. Ehri (eds) *Word Recognition in Beginning Literacy* (pp. 3–40). Mahwah, NJ: Erlbaum.

Englemann, S., Haddox, P. and Bruner, E. (1983). *Teach your Child to Read in 100 Easy Lessons*. New York: Simon and Schuster.

Fawson, P.C. and Reutzel, D.R. (2000). But I only have a basal: Implementing guided reading in the early grades. *Reading Teacher*, 54 (1): 84–97.

Feagans, L.V. and McKinney, J.D. (1991). Subtypes of learning disability: A review. In L.V. Feagans, E.J. Short and L.J. Meltzer (eds) *Subtypes of Learning Disabilities* (pp. 3–31). Hillsdale, NJ: Erlbaum.

Fenwick, G. (1988). USSR: *Uninterrupted Sustained Silent Reading*. Reading: University of Reading.

Fields, M. and Spangler, K.L. (2000). *Let's Begin Reading Right* (4th edn). Upper Saddle River, NJ: Merrill.

Fisher, B. and Medvic, E.F. (2000). *Perspectives on Shared Reading: Planning and Practice.* Portsmouth, NH: Heinemann.

Fisher, D. and Shebilske, W. (1985). There is more that meets the eye than the eye-mind assumption. In R. Groner, G.W. McConkie and C. Menz (eds) *Eye Movements and Human Information Processing* (pp. 149–57). Amsterdam: Elsevier.

Fletcher, J.M., Morris, R., Lyon, G., Stuebing, K.K., Shaywitz, S.E., Shankweiler, D.P., Katz, L. and Shaywitz, B.A. (1997). Subtypes of dyslexia: An old problem revisited. In B. Blachman (ed.) *Foundations of Reading Acquisition and Dyslexia* (pp. 95–114). Mahwah, NJ: Erlbaum.

Flynn, J.M. and Rahbar, M. (1998). Improving teacher prediction of children at risk of reading failure. *Psychology in the Schools*, 35 (2): 163–72.

Foorman, B.R., Francis, D.J., Fletcher, J.M., Schatschneider, C. and Mehta, P. (1998). The role of instruction in learning to read: Preventing reading failure in at-risk children. *Journal of Educational Psychology*, 90 (1): 37–55.

Foorman, B.R., Francis, D.J., Shaywitz, S.E., Shaywitz, B.A. and Fletcher, J.M. (1997). The case for early reading intervention. In B. Blachman (ed.) *Foundations of Reading Acquisition and Dyslexia* (pp. 243–64). Mahwah, NJ: Erlbaum.

Fountas, I.C. and Pinnell, G.S. (1996). *Guided Reading.* Portsmouth, NH: Heinemann.

Fountas, I.C. and Pinnell, G.S. (1999). *Matching Books to Readers.* Portsmouth, NH: Heinemann.

Fowler, D. (1998). Balanced reading instruction in practice. *Educational Leadership*, 55 (6): 11–12.

Fox, B.J. (2000). *Word Identification Strategies* (2nd edn). Upper Saddle River, NJ: Merrill.

Franklyn, B. (1987). *Learning Disability: Dissenting Essays.* London: Falmer.

Freppon, P.A. and Dahl, K. (1998). Balanced instruction: insights and considerations. *Reading Research Quarterly*, 33 (2): 240–51.

Frith, U. (1985). Beneath the surface of developmental dyslexia. In K. Patterson, J. Marshall and M. Coltheart (eds) *Surface Dyslexia.* London: Erlbaum.

Fry, E. (1977). *Elementary Reading Instruction.* New York: McGraw-Hill.

Fuchs, D., Fuchs, L. and Burish, P. (2000). Peer-assisted learning strategies: An evidence-based practice to promote reading achievement. *Learning Disabilities Research and Practice*, 15 (2): 85–91.

Gagne, E.D., Yekovich, C.W. and Yekovich, F.R. (1993). *The Cognitive Psychology of School Learning* (2nd edn). London: HarperCollins.

Gambrell, L. and Dromsky, A. (2000). Fostering reading comprehension. In D.S. Strickland and L.M. Morrow (eds) *Beginning Reading and Writing* (pp. 143–53). New York: Teachers College Press.

Gaskins, I.W. (1998). A beginning literacy program for at-risk and delayed readers. In J. Metsala and L. Ehri (eds) *Word Recognition in Beginning Literacy* (pp. 209–32). Mahwah, NJ: Erlbaum.

Gaskins, I.W., Ehri, L.C., Cress, C., O'Hara, C. and Donnelly, K. (1998). Procedures for word learning: Making discoveries about words. In R.L. Allington (ed.) *Teaching Struggling Readers: Articles from* The Reading Teacher (pp. 238–56). Newark, DE: International Reading Association.

Gillet, J. and Temple, C. (2000). *Understanding Reading Problems: Assessment and Instruction* (5th edn). New York: Longman.

Gillet, S. and Bernard, M. (1989). *Reading Rescue* (2nd edn). Melbourne: Australian Council for Educational Research.

Glynn, T., McNaughton, S., Robinson, V. and Quinn, M. (1979). *Remedial Reading at Home*. Wellington: New Zealand Council for Educational Research.

Goldsworthy, C.L. (2001). *Sourcebook of Phonological Awareness Activities*. San Diego, CA: Singular Publishing.

Goodman, K.S. (1967). Reading: A psycholinguistic guessing game. *Journal of the Reading Specialist*, 6: 126–35.

Goodman, K.S. (1986). *What's Whole in Whole Language?* Portsmouth, NH: Heinemann.

Goodman, K.S. (1989). Whole Language Is Whole: A Response to Heymsfeld. *Educational Leadership*, 46 (6): 69–70.

Goodman, K.S. (1996). *On Reading*. Portsmouth, NH: Heinemann.

Goodman, K.S. (1997). The reading process. In V. Edwards and D. Corson (eds) *Encyclopedia of Language and Education* (vol. 2, pp. 1–7). Dordrecht: Kluwer.

Goodman, Y. and Burke, C. (1972). *Reading Miscue Analysis: Procedure for Diagnosis and Evaluation*. London: Macmillan.

Graham, K. and Harris, S. (1994). Implications of constructivism for teaching writing to students with special needs. *Journal of Special Education*, 28 (3): 275–89.

Graham, L. and Wong, B.Y.L. (1993). Comparing two modes of teaching a question-answering strategy for enhancing reading comprehension: Didactic and self-instructional training. *Journal of Learning Disabilities*, 26 (4): 270–9.

Graves, M.F., Juel, C. and Graves, B.B. (1998). *Teaching Reading in the 21st Century*. Boston: Allyn and Bacon.

Gunning, T.G. (2000). *Creating Literacy Instruction for All Children* (3rd edn). Boston: Allyn and Bacon.

Gunning, T.G. (2001). *Building Words: A Resource Manual for Teaching Word Analysis and Spelling Strategies*. Boston: Allyn and Bacon.

Guppy, O. and Hughes, M. (1999). *The Development of Independent Reading*. Buckingham: Open University Press.

Guthrie, J.T. and Alvermann, D.E. (1999). *Engaged Reading: Processes, Practices, and Policy Implications*. New York: Teachers College Press.

Hallahan, D.P. and Kauffman, J. (2000). *Exceptional Learners* (8th edn). Boston: Allyn and Bacon.

Hannon, P. (1995). *Literacy, Home and School*. London: Falmer.

Harp, B. and Brewer, J.A. (2000). Assessing reading and writing in the early years. In D.S. Strickland and L.M. Morrow (eds) *Beginning Reading and Writing* (pp. 154–67). New York: Teachers College Press.

Harris, K. and Graham, S. (1996). Memo to constructivists: Skills count too. *Educational Leadership*, 53 (5): 26–9.

Harrison, B., Zollner, J. and Magill, B. (1996). The hole in whole language. *Australian Journal of Remedial Education*, 27 (5): 6–18.

Harrison, C. (1996). Methods of teaching reading: Key issues in research and implications for practice. *Interchange* 39. Edinburgh: Scottish Office of the Education and Industry Department.

Hayden, R. (1998). Training parents as reading facilitators. In R.L. Allington (ed.) *Teaching Struggling Readers: Articles from* The Reading Teacher (pp. 296–9). Newark, DE: International Reading Association.

Heilman, A.W. (1993). *Phonics in Proper Perspective* (7th edn). Columbus, OH: Merrill.

Hempenstall, K. (1998). Miscue analysis, whole language, reading assessment: The Reading Miscue Inventory – A critique. *Australian Journal of Learning Disabilities*, 3 (4): 32–7.

Henry, M.K. and Redding, N.C. (1999). *Patterns for Success: A Multisensory Approach to Teaching Phonics and Word Analysis*. Austin, TX: Pro-ed.

Hockenbury, J., Kauffman, J.M. and Hallahan, D.P. (2000). What is right about special education? *Exceptionality*, 8 (1): 3–11.

Hoffman, J.V., Baumann, J. and Afflerbach, P. (2000). *Balancing Principles for Teaching Elementary Reading*. Mahwah, NJ: Erlbaum.

Hoffman, J.V. and McCarthey S.J. (2000). Our principles and our practices. In J.V. Hoffman, J. Baumann and P. Afflerbach *Balancing Principles for Teaching Elementary Reading* (pp. 11–58). Mahwah, NJ: Erlbaum.

Høien, T. and Lundberg, I. (2000). *Dyslexia: From Theory to Intervention*. Dordrecht: Kluwer.

Holdaway, D. (1982). Shared book experience: Teaching reading using favourite books. *Theory into Practice*, 21 (4): 293–300.

Holdaway, D. (1990). *Independence in Reading* (3rd edn). Sydney: Ashton Scholastic.

House of Representatives Standing Committee on Employment, Education and Training (1993). *The Literacy Challenge*. Canberra: Australian Government Publishing Service.

Howell, E.R. and Peachey, G.T. (1990). Visual dysfunction and learning. In S.R. Butler (ed.) *The Exceptional Child* (pp. 223–50). Harcourt Brace Jovanovich.

International Reading Association (IRA) (1997). *Position Statement: The Role of Phonics in Reading Instruction*. Newark: IRA.

Iversen, S. and Tunmer, W. (1993). Phonological processing skills and the Reading Recovery program. *Journal of Educational Psychology*, 85 (1): 112–26.

Jenkins, J.R. and Heinen, A. (1989). Students' preferences for service delivery: Pull-out, in-class or integrated models. *Exceptional Children*, 55 (6): 516–23.

John, K.R. (1998). Selected short-term memory tests as predictors of reading readiness. *Psychology in the Schools*, 35 (2): 137–44.

Johnson, D. (1998). Dyslexia: The identification process. In B.K. Shapiro, P.J. Accardo and A.J. Capute (eds) *Specific Reading Disability: A View of the Spectrum* (pp. 137–54). Timonium, MD: York Press.

Jones, C.J. (1998). *Curriculum-Based Assessment the Easy Way*. Springfield: Thomas.

Just, M.A. and Carpenter, P.A. (1987). *The Psychology of Reading and Language Comprehension*. Boston: Allyn and Bacon.

Kameenui, E.J. and Simmons, D.C. (1999). Beyond effective practices to schools as host environments: Building and sustaining a school-wide intervention model in beginning reading for all children. *Australasian Journal of Special Education*, 23 (2/3): 100–27.

Kaufmann, W.E. (1996). Mental retardation and learning disorders. In A.J. Capute and P.J. Accardo (eds) *Developmental Disabilities in Infancy and Childhood* (vol. 2, pp. 49–70). Baltimore: Brookes.

Kavale, K. and Forness, S. (2000). Policy decisions in special education: The role of meta-analysis. In R. Gersten, E. Schiller and S. Vaughn (eds) *Contemporary Special Education Research* (pp. 281–326). Mahwah, NJ: Erlbaum.

Kemp, M. (1987). *Watching Children Read and Write*. Melbourne: Nelson.

Kirk, S. (1962). *Educating Exceptional Children*. Boston: Houghton Mifflin.

Klesius, J.P. and Griffith, P.L. (1998). Interactive storybook reading for at-risk learners. In R.L. Allington (ed.) *Teaching Struggling Readers: Articles from* The Reading Teacher (pp. 175–86). Newark: DE: International Reading Association.

Kucera, H. and Francis, W. (1967). *Computational Analysis of Present-Day American English*. Providence, RI: Brown University Press.

Labbo, L.D. and Ash, G.E. (1998). What is the role of computer-related technology in early literacy? In S.B. Neuman and K.A. Roskos (eds) *Children Achieving: Best Practices in Early Literacy* (pp. 180–97). Newark, DE: International Reading Association.

Leslie, L. (1997). *Authentic Literacy Assessment: An Ecological Approach*. New York: Longman.

Limbrick, l., McNaughton, S. and Cameron, M. (1985). *Peer Power: Using Peer-Tutoring to Help Low-Progress Readers*. Wellington: New Zealand Council for Educational Research.

Linn, R. and Gronlund, E. (1995). *Measurement and Assessment in Teaching* (7th edn). Englewood Cliffs, NJ: Merrill.

Liubinas, J. (2000). Understanding the reading process: An optometric viewpoint. *Australian Journal of Learning Disabilities*, 5 (4): 18–21.

Lloyd, J.W. (1988). Direct academic interventions in learning difficulties. In M.C. Wang, M.C. Reynolds and H.J. Walberg (eds) *Handbook for Special Education: Research and Practice* (vol. 2, pp. 345–66). Oxford: Pergamon.

Lovett, M.W., Lacerenza, L., Borden, S.L., Frijters, J.C., Steinbach, K.A. and de Palma, M. (2000). Components of effective remediation for developmental reading disabilities: Combining phonological and strategy-based instruction to improve outcomes. *Journal of Educational Psychology*, 92 (2): 263–83.

Lyon, G.R. (1998). Why reading is not a natural process. *Educational Leadership*, 55 (6): 14–18.

McCoy, K.M. (1995). *Teaching Special Learners in the General Education Classroom* (2nd edn). Denver: Love.

McEwan, E.K. (1998). *The Principal's Guide to Raising Reading Achievement*. Thousand Oaks, CA: Corwin Press.

McGee, L.M. and Richgels, D.J. (2000). *Literacy's Beginnings: Supporting Young Readers and Writers* (3rd edn). Boston: Allyn and Bacon.

McGuinness, D. (1998). *Why Children Can't Read and What We Can Do About It*. Harmondsworth: Penguin Books.

McInerney, D. and McInerney, V. (1998). *Educational Psychology: Constructing Learning* (2nd edn). Sydney: Prentice Hall.

McIntyre, E. and Pressley, M. (1996). *Balanced Instruction: Strategies and Skills in Whole Language*. Norwood, MA: Christopher-Gordon.

Magliano, J.P., Trabasso, T. and Graesser, A.C. (1999). Strategic processing during comprehension. *Journal of Educational Psychology*, 91 (4): 615–29.

Maheady, L., Sacca, M. and Harper, G. (1987). Classwide student tutoring teams: The effects of peer-mediated instruction on academic performance. *Journal of Special Education*, 21: 107–21.

Manis, F.R., Custodio, R. and Szeszulksi, P.A. (1993). Development of phonological and orthographic skills: A 2-year longitudinal study of dyslexic children. *Journal of Experimental Child Psychology*, 56: 64–86.

Marinak, B.A. and Henk, W.A. (1999). Balanced literacy instruction in the elementary school: The West Hanover Story. In S.M. Blair-Larsen and K.A. Williams (eds) (1999). *The Balanced Reading Program* (pp. 136–71). Newark, DE: International Reading Association.

Mariotti, A.S. and Homan, S.P. (2001). *Linking Reading Assessment to Instruction* (3rd edn). Mahwah, NJ: Erlbaum.

Marston, D. (1996). A comparison of inclusion only, pull-out only, and combined services models for students with mild disabilities. *Journal of Special Education*, 30 (2): 121–32.

Marzano, R.J. and Paynter, D.E. (1994). *New Approaches to Literacy: Helping Students Develop Reading and Writing Skills*. Washington DC: American Psychological Association.

Mastropieri, M., Scruggs, T. and Butcher, K. (1997). How effective is inquiry learning for students with mild disabilities? *Journal of Special Education*, 31 (2): 199–211.

Mather, N. and Roberts, R. (1994). Learning disabilities: A field in danger of extinction. *Learning Disabilities Research and Practice*, 9 (1): 49–58.

May, F.B. (2001). *Unraveling the Seven Myths of Reading: Assessment and Reading Intervention Practices for Counteracting their Effects*. Boston: Allyn and Bacon.

Metsala, J. and Ehri, L. (eds) (1998). *Word Recognition in Beginning Literacy*. Mahwah, NJ: Erlbaum.

Miles, T.R. (1983). *Help for Dyslexic Children*. London: Methuen.

Miller, W.H. (1995). *Alternative Assessment Techniques for Reading and Writing*. West Nyack, NY: Centre for Applied Research in Education.

Montgomery, K. (2001). *Authentic Assessment: A Guide for Elementary Teachers*. New York: Longman.

Moody, S.W., Vaughn, S., Hughes, M.T. and Fischer, M. (2000). Reading instruction in the resource room: Set up for failure. *Exceptional Children*, 66 (3): 305–16.

Morrow, L.M. and Woo, D.G. (eds) (2001). *Tutoring Programs for Struggling Readers*. New York: Guilford Press.

Mosenthal, P.B. (1999). Understanding engagement: Historical and political contexts. In J.T. Guthrie and D.E. Alvermann (eds) *Engaged Reading: Processes, Practices and Policy Implications* (pp. 1–16). New York: Teachers College Press.

Moustafa, M. (2000). Phonics instruction. In D.S. Strickland and L.M. Morrow (eds) *Beginning Reading and Writing* (pp. 121–33). New York: Teachers College Press.

Munro, J. (1998). *Assessing and Teaching Phonological Knowledge*. Melbourne: Australian Council for Educational Research.

National Health and Medical Research Council (Australia) (1990). *Learning Difficulties in Children and Adolescents*. Canberra: Australian Government Publishing Service.

Neale, M.D. (1999). *Neale Analysis of Reading Ability: Manual* (3rd edn). Melbourne: Australian Council for Educational Research.

Neill, D.M. (2000). Transforming student assessment. In R.D. Robinson, M.C. McKenna and J.M. Wedman (eds) *Issues and Trends in Literacy Education* (2nd edn, pp. 136–48). Boston: Allyn and Bacon.

Nessel, D.D. and Jones, M.B. (1981). *The Language-Experience Approach to Reading*. New York: Teachers College Press.

Nicholson, T. (1991). Do children read words better in context or in lists? A classic study revisited. *Journal of Educational Psychology*, 83: 444–50.

Nicholson, T. (1994). Whole language debate continues. *The Reading Teacher*, 47 (8): 598.

Nicholson, T. (1998). Teaching reading: The flashcard strikes back. *The Reading Teacher*, 52 (2): 188–92.

Nicholson, T. (1999). Literacy in the family and society. In G.B. Thompson and T. Nicholson (eds) *Learning to Read: Beyond Phonics and Whole Language* (pp. 1–22). New York: Teachers College Press.

Nicholson, T. and Tan, A. (1999). Proficient word identification for comprehension. In G.B. Thompson and T. Nicholson (eds) *Learning to Read: Beyond Phonics and Whole Language* (pp. 150–73). New York: Teachers College Press.

Ogle, D. (1986). K-W-L: A teaching model that develops active reading of expository text. *The Reading Teacher*, 39: 564–70.

Osborne, J. and Lehr, F. (eds) (1998). *Literacy for All: Issues in Teaching and Learning*. New York: Guilford Press.

Ott, P. (1997). *How to Detect and Manage Dyslexia*. Oxford: Heinemann.

Palinscar, A.S. and Brown, A.L. (1984). Reciprocal teaching of comprehension-fostering and monitoring activities. *Cognition and Instruction*, 1: 117–75.

Pavlidis, G.T. (1981). Sequencing, eye movements and the early objective diagnosis of dyslexia. In G.T. Pavlidis and T.R. Miles (eds) *Dyslexia: Research and its Applications to Education* (pp. 99–163). Chichester: Wiley.

Perfetti, C., Beck, I., Bell, L., and Hughes, C. (1987). Phonemic knowledge and learning to read are reciprocal: A longitudinal study of first grade children. *Merrill-Palmer Quarterly*, 33: 283–319.

Phillips, N., Fuchs, L., Fuchs, D. and Hamlett, C. (1996). Instructional variables affecting student achievement: Case studies of two contrasting teachers. *Learning Disabilities Research and Practice*, 11 (1): 24–33.

Pikulski, J. (1994). Preventing reading failure: A review of five effective programs. *The Reading Teacher*, 48 (1): 30–39.

Pinnell, G.S. (1997). Reading Recovery: A summary of research. In J. Flood, S.B. Heath and D. Lapp (eds) *Handbook of Research on Teaching Literacy through the Communicative and Visual Arts* (pp. 638–54). New York: Macmillan.

Polloway, E.A. and Patton, J.R. (1997). *Strategies for Teaching Learners with Special Needs* (6th edn). Upper Saddle River, NJ: Merrill.

Pressley, M. (1991). Can learning-disabled children become good information processors? How can we find out? In L.V. Feagans, E.J. Short and L.J. Meltzer (eds) *Subtypes of Learning Disabilities: Theoretical Perspectives and Research* (pp. 137–61). Hillsdale, NJ: Erlbaum.

Pressley, M. (1998). *Reading Instruction that Works: The Case for Balanced Teaching*. New York: Guilford Press.

Pressley, M. (1999). Self-regulated comprehension processing and its development through instruction. In L. Gambrell, L.M. Morrow, S.B. Neuman and M. Pressley (eds) *Best Practices in Literacy Instruction* (pp. 90–97). New York: Guilford Press.

Pressley, M. and McCormick, C.B. (1995). *Advanced Educational Psychology for Educators, Researchers and Policy-Makers*. New York: HarperCollins.

Pressley, M., Wharton-McDonald, R. and Mistretta, J. (1998). Effective beginning literacy instruction: Dialectical, scaffolded, and contextualised. In J. Metsala and L.C. Ehri (eds) *Word Recognition in Beginning Literacy* (pp. 357–73). Mahwah, NJ: Erlbaum.

Prior, M. (1996). *Understanding Specific Learning Difficulties*. Hove: Psychology Press.

Raphael, T.E. and Pearson, P.D. (1985). Increasing students' awareness of sources of information for answering questions. *American Educational Research Journal*, 22: 217–35.

Rasinski, T. (1998). Fluency for everyone: Incorporating fluency instruction in the classroom. In R.L. Allington (ed.) *Teaching Struggling Readers: Articles from* The Reading Teacher (pp. 257–60). Newark, DE: International Reading Association.

Rasinski, T. and Padak, N. (1998). Reading wars: Nothing new. *The Reading Teacher*, 51 (8): 630–31.

Rasinski, T. and Padak, N. (2000). *Effective Reading Strategies: Teaching Children who Find Reading Difficult* (2nd edn). Upper Saddle River, NJ: Merrill.

Rayner, K. (1997). Understanding eye movements in reading. *Scientific Studies of Reading*, 1 (4): 317–39.

Rayner, K. and Pollatsek, A. (1989). *The Psychology of Reading*. Englewood Cliffs, NJ: Prentice Hall.

Rayner, K., Rayner, G. and Pollatsek, A. (1995). Eye movements and discourse processing. In R.F. Lorch and E.J. O'Brien (eds) *Sources of Coherence in Reading* (pp. 9–35). Hillsdale, NJ: Earlbaum.

Reutzel, D.R. (1999). On balanced reading. *The Reading Teacher*, 52 (4): 322–4.

Reys, R., Suydam, M., Lindquist, M. and Smith, N. (1998). *Helping Children Learn Mathematics* (5th edn). Boston: Allyn and Bacon.

Riley, J. (1999). The reading debate. In R. Nunes (ed.) *Learning to Read: An Integrated View from Research and Practice* (pp. 217–28). Dordrecht: Kluwer.

Rivalland, J. (2000). Policies and practices: Students with literacy difficulties. In W. Louden, L. Chan, J. Elkins, D. Greaves, H. House, M. Milton, S. Nichols, M. Rohl, J. Rivalland, C. van Kraayenoord (eds) *Mapping the Territory: Primary Students with Learning Difficulties in Literacy and Numeracy – Overview* (vol. 1, pp. 41–65). Canberra: Department of Education, Training and Youth Affairs.

Rivalland, J. and House, H. (2000). Mapping system provision for learning difficulties. In W. Louden, L. Chan, J. Elkins, D. Greaves, H. House, M. Milton, S. Nichols,

M. Rohl, J. Rivalland, C. van Kraayenoord (eds) *Mapping the Territory: Primary Students with Learning Difficulties in Literacy and Numeracy – Analysis* (vol. 2, pp. 125–59). Canberra: Department of Education, Training and Youth Affairs.

Roberts, G.R. (1999). *Learning to Teach Reading*. London: Chapman.

Rosenshine, B. and Meister, C. (1994). Reciprocal teaching: A review of research. *Review of Educational Research*, 64 (4): 479–530.

Rubin, D. (2000). *Teaching Elementary Language Arts: A Balanced Approach* (6th edn). Boston: Allyn and Bacon.

Rumsey, J.M. and Eden, G. (1998). Functional neuro-imaging of developmental dyslexia. In B.K. Shapiro, P.J. Accardo and A.J. Capute (eds) *Specific Reading Disability: A View of the Spectrum* (pp. 62–85). Timonium, MD: York Press.

Ryan, J. (1999). Visual processing in reading and dyslexia: A proposed relationship between WISC III coding subtest and phonological coding. In D. Barwood, D. Geaves and P. Jeffery (eds) *Teaching Numeracy and Literacy: Interventions and Strategies for 'At-Risk' Students* (pp. 19–55). Melbourne: AREA Press.

Salinger, T. (1993). *Models of Literacy Instruction*. New York: Macmillan.

Salvia, J. and Ysseldyke, J. (1998). *Assessment* (7th edn). Boston: Houghton Mifflin.

Sampson, O.C. (1975). *Remedial Education*. London: Routledge and Kegan Paul.

Samway, K.D. (1995). *Buddy Reading*. Portsmouth, NH: Heinemann.

Scarborough, H.S. (1998). Early identification of children at risk for reading disabilities. In B.K. Shapiro, P.J. Accardo and A.J. Capute (eds) *Specific Reading Disability: A View of the Spectrum* (pp. 75–107). Timonium, MD: York Press.

Schumm, J. and Schumm, G. (1999). *The Reading Tutor's Handbook*. Minneapolis, MN: Free Spirit Publishing.

Searfoss, L.W., Readence, J.E. and Mallette, M.H. (2001). *Helping Children Learn to Read* (4th edn). Boston: Allyn and Bacon.

Sewell, G. (1982). *Reshaping Remedial Education*. London: Croom Helm.

Shapiro, B.K. (1998). Specific reading disability: Splitting and lumping. In B.K. Shapiro, P.J. Accardo and A.J. Capute (eds) *Specific Reading Disability: A View of the Spectrum* (pp. 21–32). Timonium, MD: York Press.

Share, D.L and Stanovich, K.E. (1995). Cognitive processes in early reading development: accommodating individual differences into a model of acquisition. *Issues in Education*, 1 (1): 1–57.

Siegel, L.S. (1998). Phonological processing deficits and reading disabilities. In J. Metsala and L.C. Ehri (eds) *Word Recognition in Beginning Literacy* (pp. 141–60). Mahwah, NJ: Erlbaum.

Simmons, J. (2000). *You Never Asked Me to Read: Useful Assessment of Reading and Writing Problems*. Boston: Allyn and Bacon.

Slavin, R.E. and Madden, N.A. (2001). *One Million Children: Success for All*. Thousand Oaks, CA: Corwin Press.

Smith, F. (1979). *Reading without Nonsense*. New York: Teachers College Press.

Smith, N.B. (1969). The many faces of reading comprehension. *The Reading Teacher*, 23: 249–59 and 291.

Smith, S.D., Brower, A.M., Cardon, L.R. and DeFries, J.C. (1998). Genetics of reading disability: Further evidence for a gene on Chromosome 6. In B.K. Shapiro, P.J. Accardo and A.J. Capute (eds) *Specific Reading Disability: A View of the Spectrum* (pp. 63–74). Timonium, MD: York Press.

Smith-Burke, M.T. (2001). Reading Recovery: A systematic approach to early intervention. In L.M. Morrow and D.G. Woo (eds) *Tutoring Programs for Struggling Readers* (pp. 216–36). New York: Guilford Press.

Snow, C., Burns, S. and Griffin, P. (1998). *Preventing Reading Difficulties in Young Children*. Washington, D.C.: National Academy Press.

Spafford, C.S. and Grosser, G.S. (1996). *Dyslexia: Research and Resource Guide*. Boston: Allyn and Bacon.

Spiegel, D.L. (1999). Meeting each child's literacy needs. In L. Gambrell, L. Morrow, S. Neuman and M. Pressley (eds) *Best Practices in Literacy Instruction* (pp. 245–57). New York: Guilford Press.

Stahl, S. (1998). Saying the 'P' word: Nine guidelines for exemplary phonics instruction. In R.L. Allington (ed.) *Teaching Struggling Readers: Articles from* The Reading Teacher (pp. 208–16). Newark, DE: International Reading Association.

Stahl, S., McKenna, M.C. and Pagnucco, J.R. (1994). The effects of whole language instruction: An update and reappraisal. *Educational Psychologist*, 29: 175–86.

Stahl, S. and Miller, P.D. (1989). Whole language and language experience approaches for beginning reading: A quantitative research synthesis. *Review of Educational Research*, 59: 87–116.

Stanovich, K.E. (1980). Toward an interactive compensatory model of individual differences in the development of reading fluency. *Reading Research Quarterly*, 16: 32–71.

Stanovich, K.E. (2000). *Progress in Understanding Reading: Scientific Foundations and New Frontiers*. New York: Guilford Press.

Stanovich, K.E., Siegel, L.S., Gottardo, A., Chiappe, P. and Sidhu, R. (1997). Subtypes of developmental dyslexia: Differences in phonological and orthographic coding. In B. Blachman (ed.) *Foundations of Reading Acquisition and Dyslexia* (pp. 115–41). Mahwah, NJ: Erlbaum.

Stauffer, R.G. (1980). *The Language-Experience Approach to the Teaching of Reading* (2nd edn). New York: Harper and Row.

Strickland, D.S. (1990). Emergent literacy: How young children learn to read and write. *Educational Leadership*, 47 (6): 18–23.

Strickland, D.S. (1998). *Teaching Phonics Today: A Primer for Educators*. Newark, DE: International Reading Association.

Strickland, D.S. (1999). Foreword. In L.B. Gambrell, L.M. Morrow, S.B. Neuman and M. Pressley (eds) *Best Practices in Literacy Instruction* (pp. xix–xx). New York: Guilford Press.

Strickland, D.S. (2000). Classroom intervention strategies: Supporting the literacy development of young learners at risk. In D.S. Strickland and L.M. Morrow (eds) *Beginning Reading and Writing* (pp. 99–110). New York: Teachers College Press.

Stuart M., Masterson, J., Dixon, M. and Quinlan, P. (1999). Interacting processes in the development of printed word recognition. In T. Nunes (ed.) *Learning to Read: An Integrated View from Research and Practice* (pp. 105–20). Dordrecht: Kluwer.

Sulzby, E. (1991). The development of the child and the emergence of literacy. In J. Flood, J. Jensen, D. Lapp and J. Squire (eds) *Handbook of Research on Teaching the English Language Arts* (pp. 273–85). New York: Macmillan.

Swanson, H.L. (1999). *Interventions for Students with Learning Disabilities: Meta-Analysis of Treatment Outcomes*. New York: Guilford Press.

Swearingen, R. and Allen, D. (2000). *Classroom Assessment of Reading Processes* (2nd edn). Boston: Houghton Mifflin.

Talbot, V. (1997). *Teaching Reading, Writing and Spelling*. Thousand Oaks, CA: Corwin Press.

Taylor, B., Harris, L., Pearson, P. and Garcia, T. (1996). *Reading Difficulties: Instruction and Assessment*. New York: McGraw-Hill.

Teale, W. and Yokota, J. (2000). *Beginning Reading and Writing: Perspectives on Instruction*. In D.S. Strickland and L.M. Morrow (eds) *Beginning Reading and Writing* (pp. 3–21). New York: Teachers College Press.

Thompson, G.B. (1997). The teaching of reading. In V. Edwards and D. Corson (eds) *Encyclopedia of Language and Education* (vol. 2, pp. 9–17). Dordrecht: Kluwer.

Thompson, G.B. (1999). The processes of learning to identify words. In G.B. Thompson and T. Nicholson (eds) *Learning to Read: Beyond Phonics and Whole Language* (pp. 25–54). New York: Teachers College Press.

Thompson, M.E. and Watkins, E.J. (1990). *Dyslexia: A Teaching Handbook*. London: Whurr.

Tiegermann-Barber, E. and Radziewicz, C. (1998). *Collaborative Decision Making*. Upper Saddle River, NJ: Merrill.

Tierney, R.J. (2000). Literacy assessment reform: Shifting beliefs, principled possibilities, and emerging practices. In R.D. Robinson, M.C. McKenna and J.M. Wedman (eds) *Issues and Trends in Literacy Education* (2nd edn, pp. 115–35). Boston: Allyn and Bacon.

Tilstone, C., Lacey, P., Porter, J. and Robertson, C. (2000). *Pupils with Learning Difficulties in Mainstream Schools*. London: Fulton.

Tindal, G.A. and Marston, D.B. (1990). *Classroom-Based Assessment*. Columbus, OH: Merrill.

Tombari, M. and Borich, G. (1999). *Authentic Assessment in the Classroom*. Upper Saddle River, NJ: Merrill.

Topping, K. (1995). *Paired Reading, Spelling and Writing: A Handbook for Teachers and Parents*. London: Cassell.

Topping, K., Nixon, J., Sutherland, J. and Yarrow, F. (2000). Paired writing: A framework for effective collaboration. *Reading*, 34 (2): 79–89.

Torgesen, J.K. (1998). Instructional interventions for children with reading disabilities. In B.K. Shapiro, P.J. Accardo and A.J. Capute (eds) *Specific Reading Disability: A View of the Spectrum* (pp. 197–220). Timonium, MD: York Press.

Torgesen, J.K. (1999). Reading disabilities. In R. Gallimore, L. Bernheimer, D. MacMillan, D. Speece and S. Vaughn (eds) *Developmental Perspectives on Children with High-Incidence Disabilities* (pp.157–81). Mahwah, NJ: Erlbaum.

Torgesen, J.K. (2000). Individual differences in response to early intervention in reading: The lingering problem of treatment resisters. *Learning Disabilities Research and Practice*, 15 (1): 55–64.

Torgesen, J.K., Wagner, R.K. and Rashotte, C.A. (1997). Approaches to the prevention and remediation of phonologically based reading disabilities. In B.A. Blachman (ed.) *Foundations of Reading Acquisition and Dyslexia* (pp. 287–304). Mahwah, NJ: Erlbaum.

Trethowan, V., Harvey, D. and Fraser, C. (1996). Reading Recovery: Comparison between its efficacy and normal classroom instruction. *Australian Journal of Language and Literacy*, 19 (1): 29–37.

Tunmer, W.E. and Chapman, J.W. (1999). Teaching strategies for word identification. In G.B. Thompson and T. Nicholson (eds) *Learning to Read: Beyond Phonics and Whole Language* (pp. 74–102). New York: Teachers College Press.

Turner, M. (1995). Children learn to read by being taught. In P. Owen and P. Pumfrey (eds) *Emergent and Developing Reading: Messages for Teachers* (pp. 80–92). London: Falmer.

Underwood, G. and Batt, V. (1996). *Reading and Understanding*. Oxford: Blackwell.

Vacca, J.A., Vacca, R.T. and Gove, M.K. (2000). *Reading and Learning to Read* (4th edn). New York: Longman.

Valencia, S., Hiebert, E.H. and Afflerbach, P. (eds) (1994). *Authentic Reading Assessment: Practices and Possibilities*. Newark, DE: International Reading Association.

van Kraayenoord, C. and Elkins, J. (1998). Learning difficulties in regular classrooms. In A. Ashman and J. Elkins (eds) *Educating Children with Special Needs* (3rd edn, pp. 131–76). Sydney: Prentice Hall.

van Kraayenoord, C., Elkins, J., Palmer, C., Rickards, F. (2000). *Literacy, Numeracy and Students with Disabilities*. Canberra: Department of Education, Training and Youth Affairs.

Vaughn, S., Bos, C.S. and Schumm, J.S. (1997). *Teaching Mainstreamed, Diverse, and At-Risk Students in the General Education Classroom*. Boston: Allyn and Bacon.

Vellutino, F.R. (1977). Alternative conceptualizations of dyslexia: Evidence in support of a verbal deficit hypothesis. *Harvard Educational Review*, 47: 334–54.

Vygotsky, L. (1962). *Thought and Language*. Cambridge, Mass: MIT Press.

Walker, B.J. (2000). *Diagnostic Teaching of Reading* (4th edn). Upper Saddle River, NJ: Merrill.

Walker, B. and Morrow, L. (1998). *Tips for the Reading Team: Strategies for Tutors*. Newark, DE: International Reading Association.

Walmsley, S.A. and Allington, R.L. (1995). Redefining and reforming instructional support programs for at-risk students. In R.L. Allington and S.A. Walmsley (eds) *No Quick Fix: Rethinking Literacy Programs in America's Elementary Schools* (pp. 19–44). New York: Teachers College Press.

Walther-Thomas, C., Bryant, M. and Land, S. (1996). Planning for effective co-teaching: The key to successful inclusion. *Remedial and Special Education*, 17 (4): 255–65.

Warger, Eavy and Associates (1994). *Reading Assessment in Practice*. Newark, DE: International Reading Association.

Weaver, C. (1994). *Understanding Whole Language: From Principles to Practice* (2nd edn). Portsmouth, NH: Heinemann.

Weaver, C. (2000). The basalization of America: A cause for concern. In R.D. Robinson, M.C. McKenna and J.M. Wedman (2000). *Issues and Trends in Literacy Education* (2nd edn, pp. 160–4). Boston: Allyn and Bacon.

Weisberg, P. and Savard, C.F. (1993). Teaching preschoolers to read: Don't stop between the sounds when segmenting words, *Education and Treatment of Children*, 16 (1): 1–18.

Wendon, L. (1992). *Letterland* (5th edn). Barton, Cambridge: Letterland Publications.

Wepner, S.B. and Ray, L.C. (2000). Sign of the times: Technology and early literacy learning. In D.S. Strickland and L. Morrow (eds) *Beginning Reading and Writing* (pp. 168–82). New York: Teachers College Press.

Westwood, P.S. (1994). Reading and writing in the special school. *Australian Journal of Remedial Education*, 26 (1): 28–32.

Westwood, P.S. (1995). Teachers' beliefs and expectations concerning students with learning difficulties. *Australian Journal of Remedial Education*, 27 (2): 19–21.

Westwood, P.S. (1997). *Commonsense Methods for Children with Special Needs* (3rd edn). London: Routledge.

Westwood, P.S. (1998). Which intervention? Effective strategies to overcome learning difficulties. In D. Greaves and P. Jeffery (eds) *Strategies for Intervention with Special Needs Students* (pp. 177–99). Melbourne: AREA Press.

Westwood, P.S. (2000). *Numeracy and Learning Difficulties*. Melbourne: Australian Council for Educational Research.

Westwood, P.S. and Graham, L. (2000). How many children with special needs in regular classes? Official predictions vs teachers' perceptions in South Australia and New South Wales. *Australian Journal of Learning Disabilities*, 5 (3): 24–35.

Westwood, P.S. and Scott, W. (1999). *Learning Disabilities: Advocacy and Action*. Melbourne: AREA Press.

Wheldall, K. (1995). Helping readers who are behind. *Education Monitor*, 6 (1): 23–5.

Wheldall, K., Center, Y. and Freeman, L. (1993). Reading Recovery in Sydney primary schools. *Australasian Journal of Special Education*, 17 (2): 51–63.

Witt, J., Elliott, S., Daly, E., Gresham, F. and Kramer, J. (1998). *Assessment of At-Risk and Special Needs Children* (2nd edn). New York: McGraw-Hill.

Wolf, M. (1997). A provisional, integrative account of phonological and naming-speed deficits in dyslexia: Implications for diagnosis and intervention. In B. Blachman (ed.) *Foundations of Reading Acquisition and Dyslexia* (pp. 67–92). Mahwah, NJ: Erlbaum.

Wolf, M. and Bowers, P.G. (1999). The double-deficit hypothesis for the developmental dyslexias. *Journal of Educational Psychology*, 91 (3): 415–83.

Wolf, M., Pfeil, C., Lotz, R. and Biddle, K. (1994). Towards a more universal understanding of the developmental dyslexias: The contribution of orthographic factors. In V.W. Berninger (ed.) *The Varieties of Orthographic Knowledge I: Theoretical and Developmental Issues* (pp. 137–71). Dordrecht: Kluwer.

Woo, D.G. and Morrow, L.M. (2001). Introduction to tutoring issues. In L.M. Morrow and D.G. Woo (eds) *Tutoring Programs for Struggling Readers* (pp. 1–12). New York: Guilford Press.

Wright, M.B. (1999). Practical ways of developing metacognitive reading skills in junior secondary students. In P.S. Westwood and W. Scott (eds) *Learning Disabilities: Advocacy and Action* (pp. 205–18). Melbourne: AREA Press.

Yopp, R.H. and Yopp, H.K. (2001). *Literature-Based Reading Activities* (3rd edn). Boston: Allyn and Bacon.

# Index

accuracy rate when reading  86, 89
   calculation of  86
adult literacy  7, 55
affective factors:  10, 27–28, 34
   appraisal of  28, 81
alliteration  3, 6, 67, 70
alphabetic principle  5, 7–8, 30, 42, 49, 67
alphabetic stage of word identification  19, 20
analogic phonics  43
analogy: reading by  8, 16, 20, 39, 74
analytic phonics  43
assessment:  31, 59, 64, 77–94, 99, 106
   authentic;  77, 94
   checklists;  74, 79–80, 93
   criticisms of traditional forms;  77
   decoding skills;  84–85, 113–116
   diagnostic;  77, 78–79, 82, 89, 109–116
   dynamic;  81, 82
   error analysis;  80–81
   inventories;  79, 80, 93
   miscue analysis;  80
   observation;  59, 77, 79, 80, 83
   phonemic awareness;  111–112
   phonic knowledge;  113 (see also decoding skills)
   phonological skills;  2, 111–112
   procedures;  78–83
   purposes of;  78
   resources for;  93–94, 113–116
   running records;  80–81, 83, 100
   standardised;  77, 79, 81, 89
   testing;  79, 82–83, 89, 113–116
attitudes;
   towards failure;  27, 28, 49, 81, 99
   towards reading;  26, 27–28, 41, 54, 66, 79, 81, 93, 99, 104
   towards tutorial support; 28, 63, 103–104
auditive sub-type of dyslexia  36
auditory discrimination  3, 5, 43, 89
auditory skills (see also phonological awareness)  2, 36, 67–68, 111–112
authentic assessment  77, 94
automaticity;  8, 9, 19, 23, 32, 33, 37, 42, 44, 73
   importance of in reading  9, 13, 15–16, 33, 64, 71
avoidance behaviour  27, 28, 66, 98
balanced approach to instruction  ix, 11, 40, 46, 47–48, 54, 58
basal readers: criticisms of  44
basic sight vocabulary (see sight vocabulary)
benchmarks for reading  79, 90–92

big books  51–53
blending of phonemes  3, 6, 42, 68, 71, 82, 85, 111, 115
causes of reading difficulty  23, 25–38
cloze procedure  52, 57–58, 85, 93
cognitive strategies  10, 23, 81
collaborative consultation  96, 106, 107
comprehension;  9–11, 13, 20–21, 29, 32, 58, 73, 86–87, 92, 101
   assessment of;  86–87, 89, 92
   factors affecting;  10–11, 23, 96
   levels of complexity in;  21–22, 92
   processes involved in;  10–11, 23
   strategies for; 10–11, 13, 20, 22, 33, 48, 52, 58, 59, 61–62, 96
   teaching of;  48, 58, 59–62, 101
computers  84, 107–108
concepts about books  2–3
concepts about print  3, 51, 52, 69, 99
constructivist views on reading  10, 27, 87
contextual cues  14, 15, 18, 23, 32, 37, 42, 49, 51, 57, 62, 85–86
creative level of reading comprehension  21–22
critical reading  9, 21, 22, 39, 41, 52, 58, 63
cueing systems  18–19, 39
decoding skills (see also phonic skills)  5, 14, 16, 18, 27, 35, 46, 48, 69, 78, 84–85
deficit model of learning difficulty  26
dependency rate when reading  80
   calculation of  86
developmental dyslexia  33
diagnostic assessment  78–87
   key questions for;  78
   principles of;  78
   procedures for;  79–87
   purposes of;  78
difficulty level of text  64, 66, 80, 82, 85, 98, 104–105
digraphs  8, 20, 70, 84, 113, 115
Direct Reading–Thinking Activity (DRTA)  59–60
direct teaching  3, 5, 27, 41, 42, 44, 48, 70, 72, 96–97, 98
directionality of print  3
double-deficit hypothesis  34, 37, 101
dynamic assessment  81
dyseidetic sub-type of dyslexia  36
dyslexia;  30, 31, 33–38, 108
   definition;  33, 34, 35
   problems associated with  31, 33
   subtypes;  30, 33, 36
dysnomia  37